# The Five LOVE LANGUAGES

*How to Express Heartfelt Commitment to Your Mate*

## GARY CHAPMAN

LEARNING ACTIVITIES & LEADER GUIDE

WRITTEN BY AMY SUMMERS

LifeWay Press®
Nashville, Tennessee

Published by LifeWay Press®
© 2007 • Dr. Gary Chapman

ISBN 978-1-4158-5731-1
Item 005085884

This book is a resource in the subject area Home and Family of the Christian Growth Study Plan.
Course CG-0196

Dewey Decimal Classification Number: 306.872
Subject Heading: MARRIAGE \ LOVE

To order additional copies of this resource, WRITE LifeWay Church Resources
Customer Service; One LifeWay Plaza; Nashville, TN 37234-0113;
FAX order to (615) 251-5933; E-MAIL *orderentry@lifeway.com;*
PHONE (800) 458-2772; order ONLINE at *www.lifeway.com*;
or VISIT the LifeWay Christian Store serving you.

*Printed in the United States of America*

Leadership and Adult Publishing
LifeWay Church Resources
One LifeWay Plaza
Nashville, Tennessee 37234-0175

# Contents

# About the Author

MARRIED MORE THAN 35 YEARS to Karolyn, Dr. Gary Chapman is the man to turn to for help in improving or healing our most important relationships. His own life experiences, plus over 30 years of pastoring and marriage counseling, led him to publish his first book in the Love Language series, *The Five Love Languages: How to Express Heartfelt Commitment to Your Mate.* Millions of readers credit this continual best-seller with saving their marriages by showing them simple and practical ways to communicate their love to their partner.

Since the success of his first book, Dr. Chapman has expanded his Five Love Languages series to specifically reach out to teens, singles, men, and children (coauthored with Dr. Ross Campbell).

He is the author of numerous other books, including *Five Signs of a Loving Family, The Four Seasons of Marriage, Anger: Handling a Powerful Emotion in a Healthy Way, The Five Languages of Apology,* and *Hope for the Separated.* Dr. Chapman travels the world presenting seminars, and his nationally syndicated radio program airs on over 100 stations.

Dr. Chapman also serves as senior associate pastor at Calvary Baptist Church in Winston-Salem, North Carolina. He and his wife have two grown children and currently live in Winston-Salem, North Carolina.

AMY SUMMERS wrote the learning activities and leader guide for this study. Amy's primary career is chauffeur and social secretary for her children Aaron, Rachel, and Philip. She is also an experienced writer and Sunday School leader. In addition to her parenting and writing responsibilities, Amy works part-time as a writing tutor at the local elementary school. She is a graduate of Baylor University and Southwestern Baptist Theological Seminary. She and her husband, Stephen, raise their children in Arden, North Carolina.

# About the Study

WELCOME TO *THE FIVE LOVE LANGUAGES*![1] Before you begin your study, there are a couple of things I would like to point out. First of all, this book is designed for individual study in preparation for a small-group meeting each week. You will benefit most from the material if you study a portion each day rather than trying to complete all the material for the week at one sitting. This will give you more time to concentrate on the message and what it has to say to you. The personal learning activities are designed to help you apply to your life what you are learning. Please don't skip over these activities. They will also prepare you for your small-group session where you will be asked to share some of your responses.

Consider the following suggestions to make your study more meaningful:
- Release your mind and heart. Be willing to step out of your comfort zone as you learn how to best express your love for your spouse.
- Pray sincerely both alone and with others that you will be open to how to best love your spouse through his or her love language.
- Keep a journal of things you learn throughout your study. Your memory will not always recall these things, but your journal will!
- Share freely with others what you are learning. Listen as others share their experiences as well. You can learn valuable things from each other.

Dr. Chapman said, "I have not written this book as an academic treatise to be stored in the libraries of colleges and universities. I have written not to those who are studying marriage but to those who are married, to those who have experienced the 'in love' euphoria. I have written to those who entered marriage with lofty dreams of making each other supremely happy but in the reality of day-to-day life are in danger of losing that dream entirely. It is my hope that thousands of those couples will not only rediscover their dream but will see the path to making their dreams come true."

[1]The content for this workbook comes from The Five Love Languages by Gary Chapman, Moody Press, Chicago, IL, ©1992.

*"Love is something you do for someone else, not something you do for yourself."*

# Learning to Speak Love

_____ is the most important word in the English language.

_____ is the most confusing word in the English language.

Inside every child is an _____.

_____ also have a love tank.

## The Five Love Languages

1. _____

2. _____

3. _____

4. _____

5. _____

Each of us has a _____ love language.

By nature, we speak _____ love language.

We have to _____ how to speak the _____ love language.

When the act doesn't come _____, it's a greater _____ of love.

Love is something you do for _____, not something you do for yourself.

## Discovering a Child's Love Language

1. Observe their _____.

2. Notice what they _____ of you most often.

3. Observe them as they _____ with other children.

WHAT HAPPENS TO LOVE AFTER THE WEDDING? The desire for romantic love in marriage is deeply rooted in our psychological makeup. Why is it that so few couples seem to have found the secret to keeping love alive after the wedding? The answer to this question is the purpose of this study.

The problem is that we have overlooked one fundamental truth: People speak different love languages. In the area of linguistics, there are major language groups. Most of us grow up learning the language of our parents and siblings, which becomes our primary, or native, tongue. Later we may learn additional languages but usually with much more effort. These become our secondary languages. We speak, understand, and feel most comfortable speaking our native language. If we speak only our primary language and encounter someone else who speaks only his or her primary language, which is different from ours, our communication will be limited. We can communicate, but it is awkward. If we are to communicate effectively across cultural lines, we must learn the language of those with whom we wish to communicate.

In the area of love, it is similar. Your emotional love language and the language of your spouse may be as different as Chinese from English. No matter how hard you try to express love in English, if your spouse understands only Chinese, you will never understand how to love each other. You must be willing to learn your spouse's primary love language if you are to be an effective communicator of love.

**When it comes to expressing love to one another, I speak English and my spouse speaks:**
☐ **English—We understand each other's expressions of love.**
☐ **Spanish—I don't fully understand my spouse, but I can pick up a few love-phrases here and there.**
☐ **Chinese—My spouse is trying to tell me something, but I have no idea what he or she is saying.**
☐ **Martian—My spouse and I are on completely different planets.**

My conclusion after 30 years of marriage counseling is that there are basically 5 emotional love languages—5 ways people speak and understand emotional love. In the field of linguistics, a language may have numerous dialects or variations. Similarly, within the five basic emotional love languages, there are many dialects.

The number of ways to express love within a love language is limited only by one's imagination. The important thing is to speak the love language of your spouse.

Seldom do a husband and wife have the same primary emotional love language. We tend to speak our primary love language, and we become confused when our spouses don't understand what we are communicating. We are expressing our love, but the message does not come through because we are speaking what, to them, is a foreign language. Therein lies the fundamental problem, and it is the purpose of this study to offer a solution.

Once we identify and learn to speak our spouse's primary love language, we will have discovered the key to a long-lasting, loving marriage. Love need not ~~evaporate~~ rate after the wedding, but in order to keep it alive most of us will have to put forth the effort to learn a secondary love language. We cannot rely on our native tongue if our spouses don't understand it. If we want them to feel the love we are trying to communicate, we must express it in their primary love language.

## Keeping the Love Tank Full

Psychologists have concluded that the need to feel loved is a primary human emotional need. Child psychologists affirm that every child has certain basic emotional needs that must be met if he is to be emotionally stable. Among those emotional needs, none is more basic than the need for love and affection, the need to sense that he or she belongs and is wanted. With an adequate supply of affection, the child will likely develop into a responsible adult. Without that love, he or she will be emotionally and socially retarded.

Dr. Ross Campbell, a psychiatrist who specializes in the treatment of children and adolescents says, "Inside every child is an 'emotional tank' waiting to be filled with love. When a child really feels loved, he will develop normally but when the love tank is empty, the child will misbehave. Much of the misbehavior of children is motivated by the cravings of an empty 'love tank.'"

The emotional need for love is not simply a childhood phenomenon. That need follows us into adulthood and into marriage. We needed love before we "fell in love," and we will need it as long as we live. The purpose of this study is to focus on the kind of love that is essential to our emotional health.

*At the heart of mankind's existence is the desire to be intimate and to be loved by another.*

Could it be that deep inside hurting couples exists an invisible "emotional love tank" with its gauge on empty? Could the misbehavior, withdrawal, harsh words, and critical spirit occur because of that empty tank? If we could find a way to fill it, could the marriage be reborn? With a full tank would couples be able to create an emotional climate where it is possible to discuss differences and resolve conflicts? Could that tank be the key that makes marriage work?

I am convinced that keeping the emotional love tank full is as important to a marriage as maintaining the proper oil level is to an automobile. Running your marriage on an empty love tank may cost you even more than trying to drive your car without oil. What you are about to read has the potential of saving thousands of marriages and can even enhance the emotional climate of a good marriage. Whatever the quality of your marriage now, it can always be better.

**Below are two love tanks. Draw a needle on your love tank to signify how much your craving for love is being fulfilled by your spouse. Draw a needle on your spouse's love tank to signify how well you think you are fulfilling his or her need to be loved.**

MY LOVE TANK

MY SPOUSE'S LOVE TANK

**Compare your responses with your spouse's responses. Ask God to use this study to help you and your spouse fill each others' love tanks to full and overflowing!**

# Learning the Five Love Languages

In weeks 2-6 we will look in depth at the five love languages. Here I will simply provide a brief introduction to each.

## Words of Affirmation

Mark Twain once said, "I can live for two months on a good compliment." Verbal appreciation speaks powerfully to persons whose primary love language is words of affirmation. Simple statements such as, "You look great in that suit." or "You must be the best baker in the world! I love your oatmeal cookies." are sometimes all a person needs to hear to feel loved. Another way to communicate through words of affirmation is to offer encouragement.

## Quality Time

Quality time is more than mere proximity. It's about focusing all your energy on your mate. A husband watching sports while talking to his wife is *not* spending quality time with her. Unless all of your attention is focused on your mate, even an intimate dinner for two can come and go without a minute of quality time being shared.

Quality conversation is very important to a healthy relationship. It involves sharing experiences, thoughts, feelings and desires in a friendly, uninterrupted context. Quality activities are also a very important part of quality time. Many mates feel most loved when they spend physical time together, doing activities they love to do.

## Receiving Gifts

Some individuals respond well to visual symbols of love. If you speak this love language, you are more likely to treasure any gift as an expression of love and devotion. People who speak this love language often feel that a lack of gifts represents a lack of love from their mate. Luckily, this love language is one of the easiest to learn.

These gifts need not come every day or even every week. They don't even need to cost a lot of money. Free, frequent, expensive, or rare, if your mate relates to the language of receiving gifts, any visible sign of your love will leave your spouse feeling happy and secure in your relationship.

11

## Acts of Service

Sometimes doing simple chores around the house can be an undeniable expression of love. Even simple things like laundry and taking out the trash require some form of planning, time, effort, and energy. Just as Jesus demonstrated when He washed the feet of His disciples, doing humble chores can be a very powerful expression of love and devotion to your mate.

Even when couples help each other around the house, they may still fight because they are unknowingly communicating with each other in two different dialects. It is important to learn your mate's dialect and to work hard to understand what acts of service will show your love.

## Physical Touch

Many mates feel the most loved when they receive physical contact from their partner. For a mate who speaks this love language loudly, physical touch can make or break the relationship.

Sexual intercourse makes many mates feel secure and loved in a marriage. However, it is only one dialect of physical touch. It is important to learn how your mate speaks the physical touch language. Take the time to learn the touches your mate likes. They can be big acts, such as back massages or lovemaking, or little acts such as touches on the cheek or a hand on the shoulder. It's important to learn how your mate responds to touch. That is how you will make the most of this love language.

## Discovering Your Primary Love Language

Discovering the primary love language of your spouse is essential if you are to keep his or her emotional love tank full. But first you need to discover your own love language. Having heard the five emotional love languages, some individuals will know instantaneously their own primary love language and that of their spouse. For others, it will not be that easy. Several methods can be used to help determine your love language as well as the love language of your spouse.

## Ask Key Questions

### What Makes Me Feel Most Loved By My Spouse?

What do you desire above all else? If the answer does not leap to your mind immediately, perhaps it will help to look at the negative use of love languages. What does your spouse do or say or fail to do or say that hurts you deeply? If your deepest pain is the critical, judgmental words of your spouse, then perhaps your love language is words of affirmation. If your primary love language is used negatively by your spouse—that is, he does the opposite—it will hurt you more deeply because not only is he neglecting to speak your primary love language, he is actually using that language as a knife to your heart.

### What Have I Most Often Requested of My Spouse?

Whatever you have most requested is probably in keeping with your primary love language. Those requests may have been interpreted by your spouse as nagging. They have been, in fact, your efforts to secure emotional love from your spouse.

### How Do I Express Love to My Spouse?

Chances are what you are doing for her is what you wish she would do for you. If you are constantly doing acts of service for your spouse, perhaps (although not always) that is your love language. If words of affirmation speak love to you, chances are you will use them in speaking love to your spouse.

But remember, that approach is only a possible clue to your love language; it is not an absolute indicator. For example, the husband who learned from his father to express love to his wife by giving her nice gifts expresses his love to his wife by doing what his father did, yet receiving gifts is not his primary love language. He is simply doing what he was trained to do by his father.

**After reviewing the five love languages and considering the three key questions, write below what you think is:**

**your primary love language** _____

**your spouse's primary love language** _____

13

## *Love Is a Choice*

If our spouses have learned to speak our primary love language, our need for love will continue to be satisfied. If, on the other hand, they don't speak our love language, our tanks will slowly drain and we will no longer feel loved. Meeting my wife's need for love is a choice I make each day. If I know her primary love language and choose to speak it, her deepest emotional need will be met and she will feel secure in my love. If she does the same for me, my emotional needs are met and both of us live with full love tanks.

Perhaps you are thinking, *What if the love language of my spouse is something that doesn't come naturally for me?* I am often asked this question at my marriage seminars, and my answer is, "So?"

My wife's love language is acts of service. One of the things I do for her regularly as an act of love is to vacuum the floors. Do you think vacuuming floors comes naturally for me? My mother used to make me vacuum. I couldn't go play ball on Saturday until I finished vacuuming the entire house. In those days I said to myself, *When I get out of here, I am not going to vacuum houses. I'll get myself a wife to do that.*

But I vacuum our house now. And there is only one reason. Love. You couldn't pay me enough to vacuum a house, but I do it for love. When an action doesn't come naturally to you, it is a greater expression of love. Ultimately, comfort is not the issue. We are talking about love, and love is something you do for someone else, not something you do for yourself. Love is a choice.

Marriage is designed to meet that need for intimacy and love. That is why the ancient biblical writings spoke of the husband and wife becoming "one flesh." That did not mean that individuals would lose their identity; it meant that they would enter into each other's lives in a deep and intimate way. The New Testament writers challenged both the husband and the wife to love each other. From Plato to Peck, writers have emphasized the importance of love in marriage.

Something in our nature cries out to be loved by another. Isolation is devastating to the human psyche. That is why solitary confinement is considered the cruelest of punishments. At the heart of mankind's existence is the desire to be intimate and to be loved by another.

> *When an action doesn't come naturally to you, it is a greater expression of love.*

> **For this reason a man will leave his father and mother and be joined to his wife, and the two will become one flesh.**
> Ephesians 5:31, HCSB

**Read Genesis 2:18 in your Bible. What did God Himself declare after He created the first man, Adam?**

_____

**Read Ecclesiastes 4:9-12 in the margin. Summarize these verses to explain why we all have a deep desire to be loved and intimate with another.**

_____

_____

_____

_____

_____

_____

Two are better than one, because they have a good return for their work: If one falls down, his friend can help him up. But pity the man who falls and has no one to help him up! Also, if two lie down together, they will keep warm. But how can one keep warm alone? Though one may be overpowered, two can defend themselves. A cord of three strands is not quickly broken.
ECCLESIASTES 4:9-12

## Discovering a Child's Love Language

As a parent you are responsible for filling your children's love tank. You do this best by understanding their love language and communicating to them by speaking their language. Throughout the course of this study as we focus on each of the love languages individually, there will be helps for you to discover and learn to speak your child's love language. Here are some things you can do to help you in this process:

• Observe their behavior.
• Notice what they request of you most often.
• Observe them as they play with other children.

# Take the Five Love Languages Profile

You may think you already know your primary love language. Then again, you may have no clue. The Five Love Languages Profile will help you know for certain which love language is yours.

Using these approaches will enable you to determine your primary love language. If two languages seem to be equal for you, that is, both speak loudly to you, then perhaps you are bilingual. If so, you make it easier on your spouse. He or she has two choices, either of which will strongly communicate love to you.

Two kinds of people may have difficulty discovering their primary love language. The first is the individual whose emotional love tank has been full for a long time. Her spouse has expressed love in many ways, and she is not certain which of those ways makes her feel most loved. She simply knows she is loved. The second is the individual whose love tank has been empty for so long that he doesn't remember what makes him feel loved. In either case, go back to the experience of falling in love and ask yourself, "What did I like about my spouse in those days? What did he do or say that made me desire to be with him?" If you can conjure up those memories, it will give you some idea of your primary love language. Another approach would be to ask yourself, "What would be an ideal spouse to me? If I could have the perfect mate, what would she be like?" Your picture of a perfect mate should give you some idea of your primary love language.

# How to Use the Five Love Languages Profile

Words of Affirmation, Quality Time, Receiving Gifts, Acts of Service, or Physical Touch? Which of these is your primary love language? The following profile will help you know for sure. Then you and your spouse can discuss your respective love languages and use this information to improve your marriage!

The profile consists of 30 pairs of statements. You can only pick one statement in each pair as the one that best represents your desire. Read each pair of statements and then circle the letter that matches the statement you choose. It may be tough at times to decide between two statements, but you should only choose one per pair to ensure the most accurate profile results. Once you've finished making your selections, go back and count the number of times you circled each individual letter. List the results in the appropriate spaces at the end of the profile. Your primary love language is the one that receives the most points.

Take the profile when you are relaxed and not pressed for time. Do not take the profile immediately after a disagreement with your spouse. Choose a time when you are in a fairly good mood and have a sincere desire to learn something about yourself which may enhance the emotional climate of your marriage.

# The Five Love Languages Profile

1. I like to receive notes of affirmation from my spouse.    A

   I like it when my spouse hugs me.    E

2. I like to be alone with my spouse.    B

   I feel loved when my spouse gives practical help to me.    D

3. Receiving special gifts from my spouse makes me happy.    C

   I enjoy long trips with my spouse.    B

4. I feel loved when my spouse does things to help me.    D

   I feel loved when my spouse touches me.    E

5. I feel loved when my spouse puts his/her arm around me.    E

   I know my spouse loves me because he/she surprises me with gifts.    C

6. I like going most anywhere with my spouse.    B

   I like to hold my spouse's hand.    E

7. I value the gifts my spouse gives me.    C

   I love to hear my spouse say he/she loves me.    A

8. I like for my spouse to sit close to me.    E

   My spouse tells me I look good, and I like that.    A

9. Spending time with my spouse makes me happy.    B

   Even the smallest gift from my spouse is important to me.    C

10. I feel loved when my spouse tells me he/she is proud of me.    A

    I know my spouse loves me when he/she helps me.    D

11. No matter what we do, I love doing things with my spouse.    B

    Supportive comments from my spouse make me feel good.    A

12. Little things my spouse does for me mean more than things he/she says.  D

    I love to hug my spouse.  E

13. My spouse's praise means a lot to me.  A

    It means a lot to me that my spouse gives me gifts I really like.  C

14. Just being around my spouse makes me feel good.  B

    I love it when my spouse touches me often.  E

15. My spouse's reactions to my accomplishments are so encouraging.  A

    It means a lot when my spouse helps with something I know he/she hates.  D

16. I never get tired of my spouse's kisses.  E

    I love that my spouse shows real interest in things I like to do.  B

17. I can count on my spouse to help me with projects.  D

    I still get excited when opening a gift from my spouse.  C

18. I love for my spouse to compliment my appearance.  A

    I love that my spouse listens to me and respects my ideas.  B

19. I can't help but touch my spouse when he/she is close by.  E

    My spouse sometimes runs errands for me, and I appreciate that.  D

20. My spouse deserves an award for all the things he/she does to help me.  D

    I'm sometimes amazed at how thoughtful my spouse's gifts to me are.  C

21. I love having my spouse's undivided attention.  B

    It makes me feel good when my spouse does some act of service for me.  D

22. I look forward to seeing what my spouse gives me for my birthday.  C

    I never get tired of hearing my spouse tell me I am important to him/her.  A

23. My spouses lets me know he/she loves me by giving me gifts.    C

     My spouse shows love by helping me without me having to ask.    D

24. My spouse doesn't interrupt me when I'm talking, and I like that.    B

     I never get tired of receiving gifts from my spouse.    C

25. My spouse is good about asking how he/she can help when I'm tired.    D

     It doesn't matter where we go, I just like going places with my spouse.    B

26. I love when my spouse kisses me unexpectedly.    E

     I love surprise gifts from my spouse.    C

27. My spouse's encouraging words give me confidence.    A

     I love to watch movies with my spouse.    B

28. I couldn't ask for any better gifts than the ones my spouse gives me.    C

     I love that my spouse can't keep his/her hands off me.    E

29. It means a lot when my spouse helps me despite being busy.    D

     It makes me feel good when my spouse tells me he/she appreciates me.    A

30. I love hugging and kissing my spouse after we've been apart for awhile.    E

     I love hearing my spouse tell me he/she believes in me.    A

A: _____     B: _____     C: _____     D: _____     E: _____

A = Words of Affirmation
B = Quality Time
C = Receiving Gifts
D = Acts of Service
E = Physical Touch

# Interpreting and Using Your Profile Score

Your primary love language is the one that received the highest score. You are "bilingual" and have two primary love languages if point totals are equal for any two love languages. If your second highest scoring love language is close in score but not equal to your primary love language, then this simply means both expressions of love are important to you. The highest possible score for any one love language is 12.

You may have scored certain love languages more highly than others, but do not dismiss those other languages as insignificant. Your spouse may express love in those ways, and it will be helpful to you to understand this about him or her. In the same way, it will benefit your spouse to know your love language and express affection for you in ways you interpret as love. Every time you or your spouse speak each other's language, you score emotional points with one another. Of course, this isn't a game with a scorecard! The payoff of speaking each other's love language is a greater sense of connection. This translates into better communication, increased understanding, and, ultimately, improved romance.

"The object of love is not getting something you want but doing something for the well-being of the one you love."

# Words of Affirmation

Words of Affirmation means giving your spouse words that _____.

## Dialects of Words of Affirmation

1. _____

2. _____

3. _____

4. _____

When you make a request, you are _____ your spouse.

## How to Learn to Speak Words of Affirmation

1. Make a list of _____ about your spouse.

2. Write one sentence _____ for each of those things.

3. Pick one thing from your list and _____ with your spouse.

## How do you come up with ideas of what to say?

1. Write down words of affirmation you _____.

2. Write down words of affirmation you _____.

**The tongue has the power of life and death.**
PROVERBS 18:21

PSYCHOLOGIST WILLIAM JAMES said that possibly the deepest human need is the need to feel appreciated. Words of affirmation will meet that need in many individuals. Within that love language of words of affirmation are many dialects. We will discuss a few, but there are many more. All of the dialects have in common the use of words to affirm one's spouse.

A number of biblical characters who exhibited words of affirmation as a primary love language come to mind. King David's use of praise language in the Psalms are an example of worship that affirms God's worthiness, One who is worthy of our praise. A New Testament character known for words of affirmation is Barnabas. In fact, his name meant "son of encouragement." If you follow sightings of Barnabas throughout the book of Acts, you see him verbally and by his actions, affirm the worth of individuals (Acts 4:36-37; 9:26-30; 11:19-30; 12:25; 13:1-3; 15:1-41).

**Reckless words pierce like a sword, but the tongue of the wise brings healing.**
PROVERBS 12:18

**An anxious heart weighs a man down, but a kind word cheers him up.**
PROVERBS 12:25

## Words That Build Up

Many couples have never learned the power of verbally affirming each other. One way to express love emotionally is to use words that build up.

**Read in the margin what Solomon wrote about words. Use principles from these Scriptures to contrast positive and negative effects of words on the chart below.**

**The tongue that brings healing is a tree of life, but a deceitful tongue crushes the spirit.**
PROVERBS 15:4

| POSITIVE | NEGATIVE |
|---|---|
|  |  |

Verbal compliments, or words of appreciation, are powerful communicators of love. They are best expressed in simple, straightforward statements of affirmation, such as:

"You look sharp in that suit."

"Do you ever look nice in that dress! Wow!"

"You must be the best potato cook in the world. I love these potatoes."

"I really appreciate your washing the dishes tonight."

"Thanks for getting the baby-sitter lined up. I don't take that for granted."

"I really appreciate your taking the garbage out."

**What do you think might happen to the emotional climate of a marriage if a husband and wife heard such words of affirmation regularly?**

I am not suggesting verbal flattery in order to get your spouse to do something you want. The object of love is not getting something you want but doing something for the well-being of the one you love. It is a fact, however, that when we receive affirming words we are far more likely to be motivated to reciprocate and do something our spouse desires.

> From the fruit of his lips a man is filled with good things as surely as the work of his hands rewards him.
>
> PROVERBS 12:14

**Read Proverbs 12:14 in the margin. Describe how "fruit" in this passage may be comparable to words of affirmation.**

**What kind of fruit most often comes from your lips toward your spouse? (Circle one.)**

Sweet    Nourishing    Sour    Bitter    Tasteless

**Read Hebrews 13:15 in your Bible. What is the first step to improving the quality of your "lip-fruit"?**

# Encouraging Words

Another dialect of words of affirmation to your spouse is encouraging words. The word *encourage* means "to inspire courage." All of us have areas in which we feel insecure. We lack courage, and that lack of courage often hinders us from accomplishing the positive things we would like to do. The latent potential within your spouse in his or her areas of insecurity may await your encouraging words.

**Encourage one another and build each other up.**

1 THESSALONIANS 5:11

**According to the Scriptures in the margin, what can be accomplished in our mates when we give them words of encouragement?**

_____

_____

_____

**Let us consider how we may spur one another on toward love and good deeds. Let us not give up meeting together, as some are in the habit of doing, but let us encourage one another.**

HEBREWS 10:24-25

**How often should we speak encouraging words to our mates?**

_____

**Encourage one another daily, as long as it is called Today.**

HEBREWS 3:13a

Perhaps your spouse has untapped potential in one or more areas of life. That potential may be awaiting your encouraging words. Your words may give your spouse the courage necessary to take that first step.

I am not talking about pressuring your spouse to do something you want. I am talking about encouraging him to develop an interest he already has. For example, some husbands pressure their wives to lose weight. The husband says, "I am encouraging her," but to the wife it sounds like condemnation. Only when a person wants to lose weight can you give her encouragement. Until she has the desire, your words will fall into the category of preaching. Such words seldom encourage. They are almost always heard as words of judgment, designed to stimulate guilt. They express rejection, not love.

If, however, your spouse says, "I think I would like to enroll in a weight-loss program," then you have opportunity to give words of encouragement. Encouraging words sound like this, "If you decide to do that, you will be a success. When you set your mind to something, you do it. If that's what you want to do, I will do everything I can to help you." Such words may give your spouse the courage to phone the weight-loss center.

Encouragement requires empathy and seeing the world from your spouse's perspective. You must first learn what is important to your spouse. Only then can you give encouragement. With verbal encouragement, you are trying to communicate, "I know. I care. I am with you. How can I help?" You are trying to show you believe in your spouse and his or her abilities.

Encouraging words may be difficult for you to speak. It may not be your primary love language. It may take great effort for you to learn this language. That will be especially true if you have a pattern of critical and condemning words, but I assure you it will be worth the effort.

*Encouragement requires empathy and seeing the world from your spouse's perspective.*

**Think about an endeavor your spouse is attempting or perhaps some untapped potential you perceive in your mate. Write an encouraging word you can give him or her.**

_____

_____

_____

**What encouraging words would you like to hear from your spouse?**

_____

_____

_____

# *Kind Words*

**Be kind and compassionate to one another, forgiving each other, just as in Christ God forgave you.**
EPHESIANS 4:32

**Read 1 Corinthians 13:4 in your Bible. What are the first two adjectives the Apostle Paul used to describe love?**

Love is _____

Love is _____

**What is the relationship between a patient attitude and kind words?**

_____

**As God's chosen people, holy and dearly loved, clothe yourselves with compassion, kindness, humility, gentleness and patience. Bear with each other and forgive whatever grievances you may have against one another. Forgive as the Lord forgave you.**
COLOSSIANS 3:12-13

Love is kind. If we are to communicate love verbally, we must use kind words. That has to do with the *way* we speak. The same sentence can have two different meanings, depending on how you say it. Sometimes our words are saying one thing, but our tone of voice is saying another. Our spouses will usually interpret our message based on our tone of voice, not the words we use.

The manner in which we speak is exceedingly important. An ancient sage once said, "A soft answer turns away anger" (Proverbs 15:1). When your spouse is angry and upset, if you choose to be loving you will not reciprocate with additional heat but with a soft voice. You will receive what he is saying as information about his emotional feelings. You will seek to put yourself in his shoes, see the event through his eyes, and then express softly and kindly your understanding of why he feels that way. If your motivation is different from what he is reading in your words and actions, you will be able to explain kindly. You will seek understanding and reconciliation. When you do this you are expressingwords of affirmation in the dialect of kind words. That is mature love—love to which we aspire if we seek a growing marriage.

**Read Ephesians 4:32 and Colossians 3:12-13 in the margin. What action**

**follows kindness in both those passages?** _____

**Underline in both passages the extent to which you are to forgive your spouse. What do you think that means?**

_____

# Humble Words

Love makes requests, not demands. In marriage we are equal, adult partners. If we are to develop an intimate relationship, we need to know each other's desires. To love each other, we need to know what the other person wants.

The way we express those desires, however, is all-important. If they come across as demands, we have erased the possibility of intimacy and will drive our spouse away. If, however, we make known our needs and desires as requests, we are giving guidance, not ultimatums. When you make a request of your spouse, you are affirming his or her worth and abilities. You are in essence indicating that she can do something that is meaningful and worthwhile to you. When, however, you make demands, your spouse will feel belittled, not affirmed. A request introduces the element of choice. Your mate may choose to respond to your request or to deny it, because love is always a choice. That's what makes it meaningful. To know my spouse loves me enough to respond to one of my requests communicates emotionally that she cares about me, respects me, admires me, and wants to do something to please me. We cannot get emotional love by way of demand. My spouse may in fact comply with my demands, but it is not an expression of love. It is an act of fear or guilt or some other emotion, but not love. A request creates the possibility for an expression of love, whereas a demand suffocates that possibility.

*When you make a request of your spouse, you are affirming his or her worth and abilities.*

**Pleasant words are a honeycomb, sweet to the soul and healing to the bones.**
PROVERBS 16:24

**List polite words or phrases that we associate with good manners.**

_____     _____

_____     _____

_____     _____

**Review your list. Do you use good manners with your spouse?**
☐ yes    ☐ no    ☐ usually    ☐ occasionally

## *Affirmation in Action*

If you are not a man or woman of words, if this is not your primary love language but you think it may be the love language of your spouse, let me suggest that you keep a notebook titled "Words of Affirmation." When you read an article or book on love, record the words of affirmation you find. When you hear a lecture on love or you overhear a friend saying something positive about another person, write it down. In time you will collect quite a list of words to use in communicating love to your spouse.

You may also want to try giving indirect words of affirmation—saying positive things about your spouse when he or she is not present. Eventually, someone will tell your spouse, and you will get full credit for love. Tell your wife's mother how great your wife is. When her mother tells her what you said, it will be amplified and you will get even more credit. Also affirm your spouse in front of others when he or she is present. When you are given public honor for an accomplishment, be sure to share the credit with your spouse. You may also try your hand at writing words of affirmation. Written words have the benefit of being read over and over again.

**Make a list in the margin of your spouse's positive traits.**

The next step is to express verbal appreciation for the things you like about your spouse. Review the positive traits. Add to the list things you notice in the weeks ahead. Twice a week select one positive trait and express verbal appreciation for it. When receiving a compliment, you should simply receive it and say, "Thank you for saying that" and not give a compliment at the same time.

**Read Proverbs 25:11 in the margin. In the apple on the following page, write specific words of affirmation you will speak to your spouse today.**

> A word aptly spoken is like apples of gold in settings of silver.
> PROVERBS 25:11

Give your mate a "golden apple" of spoken appreciation every day this week, either directly or to someone else about him or her. For some of those days you might choose to speak through a love letter, a card, or even a note on the car dashboard. Come back to this page at the end of the week and record:

- words of affirmation you spoke to your spouse.
- any words of affirmation you received from your spouse.
- if you received words of affirmation, how they made you feel.
- if you did not receive words of affirmation, how it made you feel.
- any differences you observe in yourself, your spouse, or your marriage.

_____

_____

_____

# *Love Tank Game*

MY LOVE TANK      MY SPOUSE'S LOVE TANK

What can I do to help fill my spouse's love tank?

_____

To the best of my ability, I will try to fill my spouse's love tank today.

MY LOVE TANK      MY SPOUSE'S LOVE TANK

What can I do to help fill my spouse's love tank?

_____

To the best of my ability, I will try to fill my spouse's love tank today.

MY LOVE TANK      MY SPOUSE'S LOVE TANK

What can I do to help fill my spouse's love tank?

_____

To the best of my ability, I will try to fill my spouse's love tank today.

"*Marriage is a relationship,
not a project to complete or
a problem to solve.*"

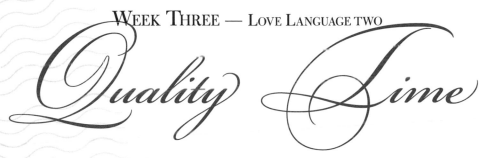

Quality time means giving your spouse your _____ _____.

## Dialects of Quality Time

1. _____

### How to Foster Quality Conversation

1. Maintain _____ _____ ,

2. Don't do anything else while you are _____.

3. Observe your spouse's _____ _____.

4. Don't _____ each other.

Quality conversation involves _____.

### Two personality types in conversation

1. _____

2. _____

2. _____

*QUALITY TIME* means giving someone your undivided attention. It doesn't mean sitting on the couch watching television together. It means sitting on the couch with the TV off, looking at each other and talking, giving each other your focused interest. It means taking a walk, just the two of you, or going out to eat and looking at each other and talking.

When I sit on the couch with my wife and give her 20 minutes of my undivided attention and she does the same for me, we are giving each other 20 minutes of life. It is a powerful emotional communicator of love.

When I share the concept of giving someone your undivided attention, I explain that it is not talking to her while you read the newspaper but looking into her eyes, giving her your full attention, or doing something she enjoys doing and doing it wholeheartedly.

**Read Song of Songs 5:6,8 in the margin. What are the indicators that her love language could be quality time?**

_____

_____

**Can you identify with the hurt and longing of this woman?** ☐ yes ☐ no

**Why?** _____

_____

_____

**Can your spouse identify?** ☐ yes ☐ no ☐ I don't know. ☐ I hope not.

Mary and Martha were sisters who followed Jesus. An encounter they had with Jesus (Luke 10:38-42) gives evidence that these two sisters spoke different love languages. Mary loved to sit at the feet of Jesus and listen to his teaching. Mary's love language was probably quality time.

I opened for my lover, but my lover had left; he was gone. My heart sank at his departure. I looked for him but did not find him. I called him but he did not answer. O daughters of Jerusalem, I charge you—if you find my lover, what will you tell him? Tell him I am faint with love.
SONG OF SONGS 5:6,8

# Togetherness

A central aspect of quality time is togetherness. I do not mean proximity. Two people sitting in the same room are in close proximity, but they are not necessarily together. Togetherness has to do with focused attention. Quality time means we are doing something together and we are giving our full attention to the other person. The activity is a vehicle that creates the sense of togetherness. Our spending time together in a common pursuit communicates that we care about each other, that we enjoy being with each other, that we like to do things together.

**List some things you could do with your spouse.**

*Togetherness has to do with focused attention.*

# Quality Conversation

One of the most common dialects of quality time is quality conversation. This means sympathetic dialogue where two individuals are sharing their experiences, thoughts, feelings, and desires in a friendly, uninterrupted context. Most who complain that their spouses do not talk mean they seldom take part in sympathetic dialogue. If your spouse's primary love language is quality time, such dialogue is crucial to his or her emotional sense of being loved.

Words of affirmation focus on what we are saying, whereas quality conversation focuses on what we are hearing. If I am sharing my love for you by means of quality time and we are going to spend that time in conversation, it means I will focus on drawing you out, listening sympathetically to what you have to say. I will ask questions with a genuine desire to understand your thoughts, feelings, and desires.

*Quality conversation means sympathetic dialogue where two individuals are sharing their experiences, thoughts, feelings, and desires in a friendly, uninterrupted context.*

**Read Proverbs 20:5 in the margin. Think of the last deep conversation you had. What did the other person do to get you to open up? (Check all that apply.)**

☐ **I've never had a deep conversation.**

☐ **He or she asked questions that helped me explore how I felt.**

**The purposes of a man's heart are deep waters, but a man of understanding draws them out.**
PROVERBS 20:5

**Tips for Being
a Good Listener**

1. Maintain eye contact.

2. Don't try to listen and do something else at the same time. Give your undivided attention.

3. Listen for feelings. Ask yourself, *What emotion is my spouse experiencing?* When you think you have the answer, confirm it. For example, "It sounds like you are feeling disappointed because I forgot ___."

4. Observe body language. Sometimes body language speaks one message while words speak another.

5. Refuse to interrupt. Your objective is not to defend yourself or to set your spouse straight. It is to understand.

☐ **He or she didn't say much at all, just listened.**
☐ **He or she showed genuine concern for me.**
☐ **Other:** _____

Many of us are trained to analyze problems and create solutions. We forget that marriage is a relationship, not a project to complete or a problem to solve. A relationship calls for sympathetic listening with a view to understanding the other person's thoughts, feelings, and desires. Most of us have little training in listening. We are far more efficient in thinking and speaking.

## *Learning to Talk*

Quality conversation requires not only sympathetic listening but also self-revelation. When a wife says, "I wish my husband would talk. I never know what he's thinking or feeling," she is pleading for intimacy. She wants to feel close to her husband, but how can she feel close to someone she doesn't know? He must learn to reveal himself. If her primary love language is quality time and her dialect is quality conversation, her emotional love tank will never be filled until he tells her his thoughts and feelings.

Self-revelation does not come easy for some of us. Many adults grew up in homes where the expression of thoughts and feelings were not encouraged but condemned. By the time we reached adulthood, we had learned to deny our feelings. We were no longer in touch with our emotional selves.

When we decide to learn the language of quality conversation, it may be like learning a foreign language. The place to begin is to get in touch with our feelings and become aware that we are emotional creatures in spite of the fact that we may have denied that part of our lives.

**Read 2 Corinthians 6:11-13 in the margin on page 39. If your spouse asks you to share what you're feeling, what is he or she really asking you to do?**

_____

_____

If you need to learn the language of quality conversation, begin by noting the emotions you feel. Three times each day ask yourself, "What emotions have I felt in the last three hours?" Write your feelings in a notepad and a word or two to help you remember the event corresponding to the feeling. Do that exercise three times a day, and you will develop an awareness of your emotional nature.

Using your notepad, communicate your emotions and the events briefly with your spouse. In a few weeks you will become comfortable expressing your emotions with him or her. Eventually, you will feel comfortable discussing your emotions toward your spouse, the children, and events that occur within the home too. Emotions themselves are neither good nor bad. They are simply our psychological responses to the events of life.

In each of life's events, we have emotions, thoughts, desires, and eventually actions. It is the expression of that process that we call self-revelation. If you choose to learn the love dialect of quality conversation, that is the learning road you must follow.

One way to learn new patterns is to establish a daily sharing time in which each of you will talk about three things that happened to you that day and how you feel about them. I call that the "Minimum Daily Requirement" for a healthy marriage. If you start with the daily minimum, in a few weeks or months you may find quality conversation flowing more freely.

**Identify one way you will seek to talk more to your spouse.**

**I will** _____

_____

**Identify one way you will seek to listen more to your spouse.**

**I will** _____

_____

_____

> We have spoken freely to you, Corinthians, and opened wide our hearts to you. We are not withholding our affection from you, but you are withholding yours from us. As a fair exchange—I speak as to my children—open wide your hearts also.
> 2 CORINTHIANS 6:11-13

# Quality Activities

Another dialect of quality time is quality activities. Quality activities may include anything in which one or both of you have an interest. The purpose is to experience something together, to feel: *He cares about me. He was willing to do something with me that I enjoy, and he did it with a positive attitude.* That is love, and for some people it is love's loudest voice.

Quality activities may include such things as putting in a garden, shopping for antiques, listening to music, going on a picnic, taking long walks, or washing the car together. The activities are limited only by your interest and willingness to try new experiences. The essential ingredients in a quality activity are: (1) at least one of you wants to do it, (2) the other is willing to do it, (3) both of you know why you are doing it—to express love by being together.

Fortunate is the couple who remembers an early morning stroll along the coast, the spring they planted the flower garden, the time they got poison ivy chasing the rabbit through the woods, the night they attended their first major league baseball game together, the amusement parks, the concerts. Those are memories of love, especially for the person whose primary love language is quality time.

**List five activities you would like to do with your spouse.**
**(Be sure to include some inexpensive activities or freebies.)**

1. _____

2. _____

3. _____

4. _____

5. _____

Compare your list with your spouse's list. Choose three activities from each list and commit to do one of those activities together once a month for six months. Record the six activities in the order in which you will do them. (Alternate the less expensive dates with the more costly ones.)

1. _____

2. _____

3. _____

4. _____

5. _____

6. _____

Where do we find time for these activities? We make time because it is just as essential to our marriage as meals are to our health. Is it difficult? Does it take careful planning? Yes. Does it mean we have to give up some individual activities? Perhaps. Does it mean we do some things we don't particularly enjoy? Certainly. Is it worth it? Without a doubt. What's in it for me? The pleasure of living with a spouse who feels loved and knowing that you have learned to speak his or her love language fluently.

**OPTIONAL ACTIVITY FOR DIE-HARD ROMANTICS:**
Think of an activity that you and your spouse both enjoy (or that he or she enjoys but you don't really care for). On a separate sheet of paper, write your spouse an invitation to engage in that activity with you, basing your invitation on the groom's summons to his bride in Song of Songs 2:10-13 (printed in the margin).

My lover spoke and said to me, "Arise, my darling, my beautiful one, and come with me. See! The winter is past; the rains are over and gone. Flowers appear on the earth; the season of singing has come, the cooing of doves is heard in our land. The fig tree forms its early fruit; the blossoming vines spread their fragrance. Arise, come, my darling; my beautiful one, come with me."
Song of Songs 2:10-13

# *Love Tank Game*

MY LOVE TANK       MY SPOUSE'S LOVE TANK

What can I do to help fill my spouse's love tank?

_____

To the best of my ability, I will try to fill my spouse's love tank today.

MY LOVE TANK       MY SPOUSE'S LOVE TANK

What can I do to help fill my spouse's love tank?

_____

To the best of my ability, I will try to fill my spouse's love tank today.

MY LOVE TANK       MY SPOUSE'S LOVE TANK

What can I do to help fill my spouse's love tank?

_____

To the best of my ability, I will try to fill my spouse's love tank today.

Notes

*"Gifts are visual symbols of love."*

# Receiving Gifts

A gift is a _____ of love.

To the individual whose primary love language is gifts, it doesn't matter

_____  _____ .

## What if gift giving doesn't come naturally?

1 Make a list of the gifts you have heard your spouse _____  _____
through the years.

2. Recruit your spouse's _____ to help you.

3. Give whatever is _____ for you to give.

4. Make a list of _____ your spouse makes about things he/she would like to have.

The gift of presence means being with your spouse in times of

_____ .

If having your spouse with you is important to you, _____ .

45

WHEN I STUDIED ANTHROPOLOGY I found that in every culture I studied, gift giving was a part of the love-marriage process.

Could it be that gift giving is a fundamental expression of love that transcends cultural barriers? Is the attitude of love always accompanied by the concept of giving? Those are academic and somewhat philosophical questions but if the answer is yes, it has profound practical implications for North American couples.

A gift is something you can hold in your hand and say, "Look, he was thinking of me," or "She remembered me." The gift itself is a symbol of that thought. It doesn't matter whether it costs money. What is important is that you thought of him or her. And it is not the thought implanted only in the mind that counts, but the thought expressed in actually securing the gift and giving it as the expression of love.

*Giving gifts is one of the easiest love languages to learn.*

Gifts are visual symbols of love. Gifts come in all sizes, colors, and shapes. Some are expensive and others are free. To the individual whose primary love language is receiving gifts, the cost of the gift will matter little. Gifts may be purchased, found, or made. The husband who stops along the roadside and picks his wife a wildflower has found himself an expression of love. The man who can afford it can purchase a beautiful card for less than five dollars. The man who cannot can make one for free.

**Add additional gift ideas to the chart below. Check the gifts you think your spouse would enjoy.**

**FREE GIFTS**
Wildflowers
Homemade card
Write a poem

**INEXPENSIVE GIFTS**
Favorite candy bar
$5.00 gift card to favorite coffee shop
Handmade item or baked good

**Read 2 Corinthians 8:12 in the margin. What is the key to making any gift a valuable expression of your love?**

_____

But what of the person who says, "I'm not a gift giver. I didn't receive many gifts growing up. I never learned how to select gifts. It doesn't come naturally for me."? Congratulations, you have just made the first discovery in becoming a great lover. You and your spouse speak different love languages. Now that you have made that discovery, get on with the business of learning your second language. If your spouse's primary love language is receiving gifts, you can become a proficient gift giver. It is one of the easiest love languages to learn.

Make a list of all the gifts your spouse has expressed excitement about receiving through the years. They may be gifts you have given or gifts given by other family members or friends. The list will give you an idea of the kind of gifts your spouse would enjoy receiving. Recruit the help of family members who know your spouse. In the meantime, select gifts you feel comfortable purchasing, making, or finding, and give them to your spouse. Don't wait for a special occasion. If receiving gifts is his or her primary love language, almost anything you give will be received as an expression of love.

**As you read Proverbs 11:24-25 in the margin, circle the description that best describes the kind of gift-giver you have been. Underline the promised blessing if you choose to learn and speak the love language of gift-giving.**

## Gifts and Money

If you are to become an effective gift giver, you may have to change your attitude about money. Each of us has an individualized perception of the purposes of money, and we have various emotions associated with spending it. Some of us have a spending orientation. We feel good about ourselves when we are spending money. Others have a saving and investing perspective. We feel good about ourselves when we are saving money and investing it wisely.

If the willingness is there, the gift is acceptable according to what one has, not according to what he does not have.
2 CORINTHIANS 8:12

One man gives freely, yet gains even more; another withholds unduly, but comes to poverty. A generous man will prosper; he who refreshes others will himself be refreshed.
PROVERBS 11:24-25

*If your spouse's primary love language is receiving gifts, then purchasing gifts for him or her is the best investment you can make.*

If you are a spender, you will have little difficulty purchasing gifts for your spouse; but if you are a saver, you will experience emotional resistance to the idea of spending money as an expression of love. You are purchasing things for yourself by saving and investing money. You are purchasing self-worth and emotional security. You are caring for your own emotional needs in the way you handle money. What you may not be doing is meeting the emotional needs of your spouse. If your spouse's primary love language is receiving gifts, then purchasing gifts for him or her is the best investment you can make. You are investing in your relationship and filling your spouse's emotional love tank. With a full love tank, he or she will likely reciprocate emotional love to you in a language you will understand. When both persons' emotional needs are met, your marriage will take on a new dimension.

**Terry is a saver and resists (at least emotionally) spending money on gifts. Stacey doesn't have a lot of money but often sacrifices personal desires to give to loved ones. Use the principles in 2 Corinthians 9:6-14 to contrast Terry and Stacey on the chart below.**

|  | **Terry** | **Stacey** |
| --- | --- | --- |
| **How do they give?** |  |  |
| **How do they receive?** |  |  |
| **With what attitude do they give?** |  |  |
| **Who benefits?** |  |  |

# The Gift of Self

An intangible gift that sometimes speaks more loudly than one that can be held in one's hand is the gift of self or the gift of presence. Being there when your spouse needs you speaks loudly to the one whose primary love language is receiving gifts. Physical presence in the time of crisis is the most powerful gift you can give if your spouse's primary love language is receiving gifts. Your body becomes the symbol of your love. Remove the symbol, and the sense of love evaporates.

**Read Proverbs 25:14 in the margin. Could this be said of you?**

_____

**Like clouds and wind without rain is a man who boasts of gifts he does not give.**
PROVERBS 25:14

**Have you insisted you are giving enough of yourself to your spouse, when actually you have been depriving him or her of your presence?**
☐ Yes   ☐ No   ☐ I'm not sure.

**What is God leading you to do in response?**

_____

_____

_____

*Physical presence in the time of crisis is the most powerful gift you can give if your spouse's primary love language is receiving gifts.*

If the physical presence of your spouse is important to you, verbalize that to your spouse. Don't expect him to read your mind. If your spouse says to you, "I really want you to be there with me," take his request seriously. From your perspective it may not be important; but if you are not responsive to that request, you may be communicating a message you do not intend.

**Complete one or both statements to indicate your desire for your spouse's presence or to offer the gift of your presence at a specific occasion or event. Share your statement(s) with your spouse.**

**I would really like you to be with me at** _____

_____

_____

**I intend to be with you at** _____

_____

_____

> Give, and it will be given to you. A good measure, pressed down, shaken together and running over, will be poured into your lap. For with the measure you use, it will be measured to you.
>
> LUKE 6:38

Almost everything ever written on the subject of love indicates that at the heart of love is the spirit of giving.

**Read Luke 6:38 in the margin. Use the logic in that verse to complete the following if/then statements.**

**If you give love, then** _____

_____

**If you measure out love sparingly, then** _____

_____

**If you give love extravagantly, then** _____

_____

# The Spirit of Giving

All five love languages challenge us to give to our spouses, but for some individuals visible symbols of love speak the loudest. Gifts need not be expensive, nor must they be given weekly. Their worth has nothing to do with monetary value and everything to do with love.

**Read 2 Corinthians 8:7 in the margin. Rewrite this Scripture into a prayer, asking God to help you learn to speak love to your spouse through giving. If you speak the love language of gifts well but would like for your spouse to demonstrate his or her love for you through gifts, pray this Scripture in regard to your spouse.**

_Just as you excel in everything—in faith, in speech, in knowledge, in complete earnestness and in your love for us—see that you also excel in this grace of giving._

2 CORINTHIANS 8:7

_____

_____

_____

_____

_____

**Exercise for the Week**
**Give gifts to your spouse at least 3 times this week. One of the gifts that you give must not require any spending of money.**

_The worth of gifts has nothing to do with monetary value and everything to do with love._

51

# *Love Tank Game*

MY LOVE TANK    MY SPOUSE'S LOVE TANK

What can I do to help fill my spouse's love tank?

_____

To the best of my ability, I will try to fill my spouse's love tank today.

MY LOVE TANK    MY SPOUSE'S LOVE TANK

What can I do to help fill my spouse's love tank?

_____

To the best of my ability, I will try to fill my spouse's love tank today.

MY LOVE TANK    MY SPOUSE'S LOVE TANK

What can I do to help fill my spouse's love tank?

_____

To the best of my ability, I will try to fill my spouse's love tank today.

*Notes*

*"Love is always freely given.*
*Love cannot be demanded."*

# Acts of Service

_____ speak louder than words.

Giving your spouse _____ about what would be a meaningful
act of service to you is important.

Make a _____ of the things you would like your spouse to do for you.

Number the items in order of _____ to you.

Listen to your spouse's _____ and you will know how to express love.

A good example of acts of service: _____ ___ _____.

The very heart of love is an attitude of _____.

SOMETIMES DOING SIMPLE CHORES AROUND THE HOUSE can be an undeniable expression of love. Doing humble chores can be a very powerful expression of devotion to your mate. We call this love language acts of service. Such actions as cooking a meal, setting a table, washing dishes, vacuuming, cleaning a commode, getting hairs out of the sink, getting bugs off the windshield, taking out the garbage, changing the baby's diaper, painting a bedroom, cleaning the garage, mowing the grass, dusting the blinds, and walking the dog are all acts of service. They require thought, planning, time, effort, and energy. If done with a positive spirit, they are indeed expressions of love.

Martha and Mary were introduced to you as sisters with different love languages in week three. Martha's love language was probably acts of service.

**Read Luke 10:38-42 and explain why Martha's love language may have been acts of service.** _____

**As you read Mark 10:43-45 in the margin, underline the reason Jesus said He came to earth.**

Jesus gave a simple but profound illustration of expressing love by an act of service. In a culture where people wore sandals and walked on dirt streets, it was customary for the servant of the household to wash the feet of the guests as they arrived. Jesus, who had instructed His disciples to love one another, gave an example of how to express that love.

**Read John 13:1-5,12-15 in your Bible. What act of service did Jesus perform?** _____

**What did He want to express to His disciples through this act of service?**

_____

**What did Jesus want His disciples to learn from His act of service?**

_____

> **Whoever wants to become great among you must be your servant, and whoever wants to be first must be slave of all. For even the Son of Man did not come to be served, but to serve, and to give his life as a ransom for many.**
> MARK 10:43-45

In most societies those who are great lord it over those who are small, but Jesus Christ said that those who are truly great will serve others.

No one likes to be forced to do anything. Love is always freely given. Love cannot be demanded. Requests give direction to love, but demands stop the flow of love.

**Look back at John 13:3-5. Why did Jesus wrap Himself with a servant's apron and kneel to wash dirty feet? (Underline your answer.)**
**He was forced to.          He chose to.          Someone suggested He should.**

**Why does it make a difference why He performed this act of service?**

_____

Make a request list. List three or four things that would make you feel loved when you get home from work. List three or four things you would really like to have help in doing, things which would help you know he loves you. When your spouse chooses to do these things for you, it is an act of love, you receive these actions as genuine expressions of love.

*Requests give direction to love, but demands stop the flow of love.*

**List things your spouse could do for you that would help you know he or she loves you.**

_____

_____

_____

**Compare your list with your spouse's list and determine whether you are making reasonable requests of one another.**

**Be honest for a moment, how do you feel about serving your spouse?**
☐ I resent it.                      ☐ I don't mind it if I'm appreciated.
☐ I just do what has to be done.    ☐ It's how I demonstrate my love.

**Read Colossians 3:23-24 in your Bible. Whether or not acts of service is your primary love language, how can this passage improve your service toward your husband or wife?**

_____

Speaking different dialects can be an issue in acts of service. This becomes apparent when the things you do for your spouse are not the most important things. That's the importance of knowing what your spouse wrote down on the previous exercise. Learning the specific dialect can be relatively easy. When speaking the right dialects, the love tank will begin to fill.

Love is a choice and cannot be coerced. Criticism and demands tend to drive wedges. Each of us must decide daily to love or not to love our spouses. If we choose to love, then expressing it in the way our spouse requests will make our love most effective emotionally.

**In the margin, you will find a portion of a letter the Apostle Paul wrote to his friend, Philemon. Read it and circle what Paul had the right to do. Underline what he did instead and why.**

**What principles from Paul's example can you apply to your marriage relationship?** _____

_____

**What criticisms do you most often receive from your spouse?**

_____

**What clues do those criticisms give you into his or her primary love language?**_____

**What will you do in response to those criticisms?**
☐ criticize back      ☐ find my love and affirmation elsewhere
☐ ignore them      ☐ find a way to answer his or her pleas for love

> **Although in Christ I could be bold and order you to do what you ought to do, yet I appeal to you on the basis of love. I then, as Paul— an old man and now also a prisoner of Christ Jesus—I appeal to you … But I did not want to do anything without your consent, so that any favor you do will be spontaneous and not forced.**
>
> PHILEMON 8-10a,14

# Doormat or Lover?

The spouse who performs acts of service out of fear, guilt, and resentment understands clearly that these are not expressions of love. A doormat is an inanimate object. You can wipe your feet on it, step on it, kick it around, or whatever you like. It has no will of its own. It can be your servant but not your lover. No person should ever be a doormat. We are creatures of emotion, thoughts, and desires. And we have the ability to make decisions and take action. Allowing oneself to be used or manipulated by another is not an act of love. You are allowing him or her to develop inhumane habits. Love says, "I love you too much to let you treat me this way. It is not good for you or me."

**Would you describe yourself as a:**
☐ **a. doormat?** ☐ **b. walker on a doormat?** ☐ **c. neither a nor b**

**If you answered either a or b, how will your behavior toward your spouse change if you commit to live by 1 John 4:18-19 (printed in the margin)?**

_____

_____

**Read Galatians 5:13-15 in the margin. Contrast the emotional climates of marriages where spouses do or do not choose to learn and speak each other's primary love language.**

| DO Choose to Learn and Speak | DO NOT Choose to Learn and Speak |
|---|---|
| | |

**Star the column that best describes your marriage.**

**Pray, asking God to empower you to serve your spouse in love and improve your marriage's emotional climate.**

> There is no fear in love. But perfect love drives out fear, because fear has to do with punishment. The one who fears is not made perfect in love. We love because he first loved us.
>
> 1 JOHN 4:18-19

> You, my brothers, were called to be free. But do not use your freedom to indulge the sinful nature; rather, serve one another in love. The entire law is summed up in a single command: "Love your neighbor as yourself." If you keep on biting and devouring each other, watch out or you will be destroyed by each other.
>
> GALATIANS 5:13-15

# Love Tank Game

MY LOVE TANK          MY SPOUSE'S LOVE TANK

What can I do to help fill my spouse's love tank?

_____

To the best of my ability, I will try to fill my spouse's love tank today.

MY LOVE TANK          MY SPOUSE'S LOVE TANK

What can I do to help fill my spouse's love tank?

_____

To the best of my ability, I will try to fill my spouse's love tank today.

MY LOVE TANK          MY SPOUSE'S LOVE TANK

What can I do to help fill my spouse's love tank?

_____

To the best of my ability, I will try to fill my spouse's love tank today.

*Notes*

*"The touch of love [takes] many forms."*

# Physical Touch

Physical touch is one of the fundamental ways of expressing _____.

Not all touches are of _____ value.

Don't assume a touch that makes _____ feel loved will make

_____ feel loved.

_____ touches require your full attention.

_____ touches take just a moment.

To touch a person's body is to touch them _____.

Physical touch in times of crisis can be the _____ you do.

If you're not comfortable with physical touch, start with something _____.

## Three questions to help you speak love to your spouse:

1. "_____?"

2. "_____?"

3. "_____?"

The key to motivation is having the _____
toward your spouse.

WE HAVE LONG KNOWN THAT PHYSICAL TOUCH is a way of communicating emotional love. Babies who are held, hugged, and kissed develop a healthier emotional life than those who are left for long periods of time without physical contact. The importance of touching children is not a modern idea. Wise parents, in any culture, are touching parents.

Physical touch is also a powerful vehicle for communicating marital love. Holding hands, kissing, embracing, and sexual intercourse are all ways of communicating emotional love to one's spouse. For some individuals, physical touch is their primary love language. Without it they feel unloved. With it their emotional tank is filled, and they feel secure in the love of their spouse.

**On the continuum below, write your initials to indicate how important daily physical touch is to you. Write your spouse's initials to indicate how important you think daily physical touch is to your spouse.**

*not at all*                                *absolutely vital*

**Compare your response with your spouse's response. Were you surprised?**
☐ **Yes**   ☐ **No**

**Why?** _____

**Evaluate how you seek to demonstrate love to your spouse. Is it possible you are providing substitutes out of your own comfort zone when what your spouse really desires is a loving touch from you?**
☐ **Yes**     ☐ **No**     ☐ **I'm not sure.**

**If you answered "yes," name one way you will show your spouse love through physical touch today.**

_____

Sexual intercourse is only one dialect in the love language of physical touch. In marriage, the touch of love may take many forms. Since touch receptors are located throughout the body, lovingly touching your spouse almost anywhere can be an expression of love. That does not mean all touches are created equal. Some will bring more pleasure to your spouse than others. Your best instructor is your spouse. She knows what she perceives as a loving touch. Learn to speak her love dialect. Your spouse may find some touches uncomfortable or irritating. Don't make the mistake of believing the touch that brings pleasure to you will also bring pleasure to her.

Love touches may be explicit and demand your full attention such as in a back rub or sexual foreplay, culminating in intercourse. On the other hand, love touches may be implicit and require only a moment, such as putting your hand on his shoulder as you pour a cup of coffee or rubbing your body against him as you pass in the kitchen. Explicit love touches obviously take more time, not only in actual touching but in developing your understanding of how to communicate love to your spouse in this way.

Implicit love touches require little time but much thought, especially if physical touch is not your primary love language and if you did not grow up in a "touching" family. Sitting close to each other on the couch as you watch your favorite television program requires no additional time but may communicate your love loudly. Touching your spouse as you walk through the room where he is sitting takes only a moment. Touching each other when you leave the house and again when you return may involve only a brief kiss or hug but will speak volumes to your spouse.

You are limited only by your imagination on ways to express love. Coming up with new ways and places to touch can be an exciting challenge. If you have not been an "under-the-table toucher," you might find it will add a spark to dining out. If you are not accustomed to holding hands in public, you may find you can fill your spouse's emotional love tank as you stroll through the parking lot. If you don't normally kiss as soon as you get into the car together, doing so may greatly enhance your travels. Hugging your spouse before she goes shopping may not only express love, it may bring her home sooner. Try new touches in new places and let your spouse give you feedback on whether he finds it pleasurable or not. Remember, you are learning to speak his language.

Let him kiss me with the kisses of his mouth … His left arm is under my head, and his right arm embraces me … How beautiful you are and how pleasing, O love, with your delights! Your stature is like that of the palm, and your breasts like clusters of fruit. I said, "I will climb the palm tree; I will take hold of its fruit." May your breasts be like the clusters of the vine, the fragrance of your breath like apples, and your mouth like the best wine. May the wine go straight to my lover, flowing gently over lips and teeth.

SONG OF SONGS 1:2; 2:6; 7:6-9

Read the Song of Songs passage in the margin. **What is your first response after reading how a biblical husband and wife spoke love to each other?**

☐ *That's* **in the Bible?**

☐ **You mean it's OK to express love through physical touch?**

☐ **I want to be freer in speaking love to my spouse through physical touch.**

☐ **Now that's my kind of love language!**

## *The Body Is for Touching*

Whatever there is of me resides in my body. To touch my body is to touch me. To withdraw from my body is to distance yourself from me emotionally. In our society, shaking hands is a way of communicating openness and social closeness to another individual. When one man refuses to shake hands with another, it communicates a message that things are not right in their relationship. All societies have some form of physical touch as a means of social greeting. The average American male may not feel comfortable with the European bear hug and kiss, but in Europe that serves the same function as our shaking hands.

There are appropriate and inappropriate ways to touch members of the opposite sex in every society. Within marriage, however, what is appropriate and inappropriate touching is determined by the couple themselves, within certain broad guidelines. Clearly our bodies are for touching, but not for abuse.

**Read 1 Corinthians 7:3-5.**

**A husband should fulfill his marital duty to his wife, and likewise a wife to her husband. A wife does not have authority over her own body, but her husband does. Equally, a husband does not have authority over his own body, but his wife does. Do not deprive one another—except when you agree, for a time, to devote yourselves to prayer. Then come together again; otherwise, Satan may tempt you because of your lack of self-control.**

**How does 1 Corinthians 7:3-5 challenge you to treat your spouse's physical body?** _____

**Read Proverbs 5:15-23 below and explore the who, what, when, where, and why of this passage.**

> *Drink water from your own cistern,*
> *water flowing from your own well.*
> *Should your springs flow in the streets,*
> *streams of water in the public squares?*
> *They should be for you alone*
> *and not for you [to share] with strangers.*
> *Let your fountain be blessed,*
> *and take pleasure in the wife of your youth.*
> *A loving doe, a graceful fawn—*
> *let her breasts always satisfy you;*
> *be lost in her love forever.*
> *Why, my son, would you be infatuated*
> *with a forbidden woman*
> *or embrace the breast of a stranger?*
> *For a man's ways are before the LORD's eyes,*
> *and He considers all his paths.*
> *A wicked man's iniquities entrap him;*
> *he is entangled in the ropes of his own sin.*
> *He will die because there is no instruction,*
> *and be lost because of his great stupidity.*

*Whom* is this passage speaking to? _____

*What* are married couples commanded to do? _____

_____

_____

_____

*When* should your spouse's body satisfy you? _____

_____

_____

*Where* must married couples find love through physical touch? _____

_____

_____

*Why* are married persons to avoid adulterous relationships? _____

_____

_____

_____

_____

*Your tender touches will be remembered long after the crisis has passed. Your failure to touch may never be forgotten.*

# Crisis and Physical Touch

In a time of crisis it is often instinctive to hug one another. Why? Because physical touch is a powerful communicator of love. In a time of crisis, we need to feel loved. We cannot always change events, but we can survive if we feel loved.

The most important thing you can do for your mate in a time of crisis is to love him or her. If your spouse's primary love language is physical touch, nothing is more important than holding her as she cries. Your words may mean little, but your physical touch will communicate that you care. Crises provide a unique opportunity for expressing love. Your tender touches will be remembered long after the crisis has passed. Your failure to touch may never be forgotten.

**Record the name of someone who especially needs to receive a loving touch from you this week. Then be sure to provide that touch!**

**a squeeze on the shoulder** _____

**a gentle pat on the face** _____

**a firm hand clasp** _____

**a hug** _____

**a passionate kiss (for your spouse only!)** _____

**other:** _____

"Love touches" are the emotional lifeline of the person for whom physical touch is the primary love language. They yearn for their spouses to reach out and touch them physically.

**Indicate loving touches that you long to receive from your spouse.**

_____

_____

_____

_____

**Share your responses with your spouse. Pray, asking God to help you meet each other's need for love through physical touch.**

# *Love Tank Game*

MY LOVE TANK          MY SPOUSE'S LOVE TANK

What can I do to help fill my spouse's love tank?

_____

To the best of my ability, I will try to fill my spouse's love tank today.

MY LOVE TANK          MY SPOUSE'S LOVE TANK

What can I do to help fill my spouse's love tank?

_____

To the best of my ability, I will try to fill my spouse's love tank today.

MY LOVE TANK          MY SPOUSE'S LOVE TANK

What can I do to help fill my spouse's love tank?

_____

To the best of my ability, I will try to fill my spouse's love tank today.

*Notes*

"*Our most basic emotional need is not to fall in love but to be genuinely loved by another.*"

# Growing in Love

Being "in love" is a _____.

It all begins with the "_____."

This experience is also accompanied by _____.

"He/she is _____!"

"_____ is more important than him/her!"

"I will _____ be happy if we aren't together!"

## Dangers of the "In-Love" Experience

1. It gives us an illusion that we have an _____ relationship.

2. It blinds us to our _____.

3. It leads us to _____ conclusions.

## How does the "in love" experience contribute to divorce?

When couples come down off the high, they see their _____.

_____ lead to fighting and arguing or they lead to withdrawing.

## How can you have a good marriage?

1. Deal with the _____.

2. Learn your spouse's _____ and start to speak it.

MOST OF US ENTER MARRIAGE by way of the "in love" experience. We meet someone whose physical characteristics and personality traits create enough electrical shock to trigger our "love alert" system. The bells go off, and we set in motion the process of getting to know the person. We are on a quest to discover love. *Could this warm, tingly feeling I have inside be the "real" thing?*

We arrange for a few more "together" experiences, and before long the level of intensity has increased to the point where we find ourselves saying, "I think I'm falling in love." Eventually we are convinced it is the "real thing," and we tell the other person, hoping the feeling is reciprocal. When it is reciprocal, we start talking about marriage because everyone agrees that being "in love" is the necessary foundation for a good marriage.

At its peak, the "in love" experience is euphoric. We are emotionally obsessed with each other. We go to sleep thinking of one another. That person is the first thought on our minds when we wake. We long to be together. When we hold hands, it seems as if our blood flows together. We could kiss forever. Embracing stimulates dreams of marriage and ecstasy.

The person who is "in love" has the illusion that his beloved is perfect. Our dreams before marriage are of marital bliss: "We are going to make each other supremely happy. Other couples may argue and fight, but not us. We love each other." We know intellectually that we will eventually have differences, but we will discuss those differences openly. One of us will always be willing to make concessions, and we will reach agreement. It's hard to believe anything else when you are in love.

We have been led to believe that if we are really in love, it will last forever. We will always have the wonderful feelings that we have at this moment. Nothing could ever come between us. Nothing will ever overcome our love for each other. We are enamored and caught up in the beauty and charm of the other's personality. Our love is the most wonderful thing we have ever experienced. Some married couples seem to have lost that feeling, but it will never happen to us. "Maybe they did not have the real thing," we reason.

**Think back to when you first fell in love with your spouse. Briefly describe how you thought, felt, and acted.**

_____

_____

**Do you still think, feel, and act that way?** ☐ Yes ☐ No

**If no, when did the change begin to occur?**

**What feelings, beliefs, and expectations contributed to maturing your relationship?**

_____

**What feelings, beliefs, and expectations were naive, unrealistic, or even harmful to the growth of your marriage?**

_____

## Is the "In-Love" Experience "Real" Love?

Unfortunately, the eternality of the "in love" experience is fiction, not fact. Dr. Dorothy Tennov, a psychologist, has done long-range studies on the in-love phenomenon. After studying scores of couples, she concluded that the average life span of a romantic obsession is two years. Eventually, however, we all descend from the clouds and plant our feet on earth again. Our eyes are opened, and we see the warts of the other person. We recognize that some of his or her personality traits are actually irritating. Her behavior patterns are annoying. He has the capacity for hurt and anger, perhaps even harsh words and critical judgments. Those little traits that we overlooked when we were in love now become huge mountains. We remember Mother's words and ask ourselves, _How could I have been so foolish?_

Welcome to the real world of marriage, where hairs are always on the sink and little white spots cover the mirror; where arguments center on which way the toilet paper comes off the roll and whether the lid should be up or down. It is a world where shoes do not walk to the closet and drawers do not close themselves; where coats do not like hangers and socks go AWOL during laundry. In this world, a look can hurt and a word can crush. Intimate lovers can become enemies, and marriage a battlefield.

**Which phrase best describes your marriage?**
☐ **"in love" euphoria**
☐ **battlefield**
☐ **real world of marriage**

**Commit your marriage to God. Tell God you trust Him to make your marriage a loving partnership that pleases Him *and* you and your spouse.**

What happened to the "in love" experience? Did we really have the "real" thing? I think so. The problem was faulty information.

The bad information was the idea that the "in love" obsession would last forever. We should have known better. If people remained obsessed, we would all be in serious trouble. The shock waves would rumble through business, industry, church, education, and the rest of society. Why? Because people who are "in love" lose interest in other pursuits. That is why we call it "obsession."

The euphoria of the "in love" state gives us the illusion that we have an intimate relationship. We feel that we belong to each other. We believe we can conquer all problems. Such obsession gives us the false sense that our egocentric attitudes have been eradicated and we have become sort of a Mother Teresa, willing to give anything for the benefit of our lover. The reason we can do that so freely is that we sincerely believe our lover feels the same way toward us. We believe she is committed to meeting our needs, that he loves us as much as we love him and would never do anything to hurt us.

That thinking is always fanciful. Not that we are insincere in what we think and feel, but we are unrealistic. We fail to reckon with the reality of human nature. By nature, we are egocentric. Our world revolves around us. None of us is totally altruistic. The euphoria of the "in love" experience only gives us that illusion.

Once the experience of falling in love has run its natural course (remember, the average in-love experience lasts two years), we will return to reality and begin to assert ourselves. He will express his desires, but his desires will be different from hers. He desires sex, but she is too tired. He wants to buy a new car, but she says, "That's absurd!" She wants to visit her parents, but he says, "I don't like spending so much time with your family." He wants to play in the softball tournament, and she says, "You love softball more than you love me." Little by little, the illusion of intimacy evaporates. The individual desires, emotions, thoughts, and behavior patterns exert themselves. They are two individuals. Their minds have not melded together, and their emotions mingled only briefly in the ocean of love. Now the waves of reality begin to separate them. They fall out of love, and at that point either they withdraw, separate, divorce, and set off in search of a new in-love experience, or they begin the hard work of learning to love each other without the euphoria of the in-love obsession.

**As you read the description of "in love" infatuation below, cross out the idealistic words and write above them true descriptions of love found in 1 Corinthians 13:4-8 (printed in the margin).**

**Love is perfect, love is bliss. It does not have morning breath; it does not get tired; it is not flawed.**

**It is always charming; it never disagrees; it never gets angry; it keeps the house clean.**

**Love does not think the other person is annoying, but laughs at all jokes even when they aren't funny.**

**It is always happy, always warm, always fuzzy, always tingly. Love never fades.**

Love is patient, love is kind. It does not envy, it does not boast, it is not proud. It is not rude, it is not self-seeking, it is not easily angered, it keeps no record of wrongs. Love does not delight in evil but rejoices with the truth. It always protects, always trusts, always hopes, always perseveres. Love never fails.
1 CORINTHIANS 13:4-8a

*True love cannot begin until the "in love" experience has run its course.*

Those of us who have fallen in love and out of love will likely agree that the experience does catapult us into emotional orbit unlike anything else we have experienced. It tends to disengage our reasoning abilities, and we often find ourselves doing and saying things we would never have done or said in more sober moments. In fact, when we come down from the emotional obsession we often wonder why we did those things.

Does that mean we are destined to a life of misery with our spouse, or we must jump ship and try again? Our generation has opted for the latter, whereas an earlier generation often chose the former. Before we automatically conclude we have made the better choice, perhaps we should examine the data. Presently 40 percent of first marriages in this country end in divorce. Sixty percent of second marriages and 75 percent of third marriages end the same way. The prospect of a happier marriage the second and third time around is not substantial.

Research seems to indicate that there is a third and better alternative: We can recognize the in-love experience for what it was—a temporary emotional high—and now pursue "real love" with our spouses. That kind of love is emotional in nature but not obsessional. It is a love that unites reason and emotion. It involves an act of the will and requires discipline, and it recognizes the need for personal growth. Our most basic emotional need is not to fall in love but to be genuinely loved by another, to know a love that grows out of reason and choice, not instinct. I need to be loved by someone who chooses to love me, who sees in me something worth loving.

**This is how we know what love is: Jesus Christ laid down his life for us. And we ought to lay down our lives for our brothers. … Dear children, let us not love with words or tongue but with actions and in truth.** 1 JOHN 3:16,18

That kind of love requires effort and discipline. It is the choice to expend energy in an effort to benefit the other person, knowing that if his or her life is enriched by your effort, you too will find a sense of satisfaction—the satisfaction of having genuinely loved another. It does not require the euphoria of the "in love" experience. In fact, true love cannot begin until the "in love" experience has run its course.

**Read 1 John 3:16,18 in the margin and complete the following statements.**

**When you are "in love" with someone you want to intertwine your life with theirs, but when you truly love someone you will:**

_____ .

**When you are "in love" with someone you declare your love with words, but when you truly love someone you also:**

_____ .

The emotional need for love must be met if we are to have emotional health. Married adults long to feel affection and love from their spouses. We feel secure when we are assured that our mates accept us, want us, and are committed to our well-being. During the in-love stage, we felt all of those emotions. It was heavenly while it lasted. But that obsession was not meant to last forever. In the textbook of marriage, it is but the introduction. The heart of the book is rational, volitional love. That is the kind of love to which the sages have always called us. That is good news to the married couple who have lost all of their "in love" feelings. If love is a choice, then they have the capacity to love after the "in love" obsession has died and they have returned to the real world. That kind of love begins with an attitude—a way of thinking. Love is the attitude that says, "I am married to you, and I choose to look out for your interests." The one who chooses to love will find appropriate ways to express that decision.

"But it seems so sterile," some may contend. "Love as an attitude with appropriate behavior? Where are the shooting stars, the deep emotions? What about the spirit of anticipation, the twinkle of the eye, the electricity of a kiss, the excitement of sex? What about the emotional security of knowing I am number one in his or her mind?" If we can learn to meet each other's deep, emotional need to feel loved and choose to do so, then the love we share will be exciting beyond anything we ever felt when we were infatuated.

**Read Song of Solomon 8:6-7 in the margin and identify the:**

commitment of true love:_____

excitement of true love: _____

staying power of true love:_____

value of true love: _____

> Place me like a seal over your heart, like a seal on your arm; for love is as strong as death, its jealousy unyielding as the grave. It burns like blazing fire, like a mighty flame. Many waters cannot quench love; rivers cannot wash it away. If one were to give all the wealth of his house for love, it would be utterly scorned.
>
> SONG OF SONGS 8:6-7

*A Personal Word*

Earlier I warned you that "understanding the five love languages and learning to speak the primary love language of your spouse may radically affect his or her behavior." Having read these pages, what do you think? Could these concepts radically alter the emotional climate of your marriage? What would happen if you discovered the primary love language of your spouse and chose to speak it consistently?

Neither you nor I can answer that question until you have tried it. Many couples who have heard this concept at my marriage seminars say that choosing to love and expressing it in the primary love language of their spouse has made a drastic difference in their marriage. When the emotional need for love is met, it creates a climate where the couple can deal with the rest of life in a much more productive manner.

**Complete the following commitment to truly love your spouse for the rest of your days.**

*My Commitment to You*

Dear _____,
*(your spouse's name)*

*I will seek*

ENDURING TRUE LOVE

*for our marriage by daily choosing*

TO DISCOVER AND SPEAK

*your love language.*

*Love,*

_____

*(your signature)*

**Think about how you can present this statement to your spouse in a way that reflects his/her love language. For example: Words of Affirmation—stare deeply into her eyes and speak it aloud; Quality Time—engage in one of his favorite activities with him and then show him your signed commitment; Receiving Gifts—easy! Write this statement in a beautiful card and deliver it with flowers; Acts of Service—do something over and above the call of duty for your spouse, and then show him this commitment you have signed; Physical Touch—you can figure that one out yourself!**

We each come to marriage with a different personality and history. We bring emotional baggage. We come with different expectations, different ways of approaching things, and different opinions about what matters in life. In a healthy marriage, that variety of perspectives must be processed. We need not agree on everything, but we must find a way to handle our differences so that they do not become divisive. With empty love tanks, couples tend to argue and withdraw. But when the love tank is full, we create a climate of friendliness, a climate that seeks to understand, that is willing to allow differences and to negotiate problems. No single area of marriage affects the rest of marriage as much as meeting the emotional need for love.

The ability to love, especially when your spouse is not loving you, may seem impossible for some. Such love may require us to draw upon our spiritual resources. A number of years ago, as I faced my own marital struggles, I rediscovered my need for God. I came to view His death as an expression of love and His resurrection as profound evidence of His power. I became a "true believer." I committed my life to Him and have found that He provides the inner spiritual energy to love, even when love is not reciprocated. I would encourage you to give your life to the One whom, as He died, prayed for those who killed Him: "Father, forgive them for they do not know what they are doing" (Luke 23:34). That is love's ultimate expression.

**Have you also become a "true believer" and committed your life to Christ?**

☐ Yes  ☐ No

**If yes, thank God for His marvelous love. If no, consider giving your life to Christ and begin a life of love you never dreamed existed!**

# *Leader Guide*

*The Five Love Languages* is designed with multiple use options to meet the needs of your group. One option for studying this material is a two-session format for a short class or retreat. If you utilize this option, you will use DVD Session 1: Learning to Speak Love and DVD Session 7: Growing in Love. You will also find the instructions for leading these sessions on the CD-ROM in your leader kit.

Another option for studying this material is to use it in a small-group setting over five to eight weeks. (Depending on the number of weeks your small group wants to study this material, you may choose to only cover Sessions 2-6 on each of the love languages, you may use Session 1 as an introduction to Sessions 2-6, or you may use Sessions 1-7.) This leader guide will provide guidance for leading seven small-group sessions with discussion and video and an optional eighth session with discussion only.

## Format of the Small-Group Session

The format of your weekly small-group time is designed to be simple but effective. Each week the sessions will break out like this:

1. The session will open with a question that allows group members to share how they are applying *The Five Love Languages* to their lives.
2. An activity or question is provided to help adults transition from a busy day to a comfort-able time of meaningful discussion with their spouse and friends.

3. Discussion starters will help guide adults to discuss the material they studied at home. (More discussion questions are offered each week than you will be able to cover in a single session. Be flexible. Consider the personality of your group as you make decisions about what topics to discuss.)

4. Couples will have a time to discuss questions you give them during the session. (Questions are listed in this leader guide or you can print copies of "Couple Discussion Questions" from the CD-ROM to pass out to couples.)

5. The group will watch a video message from Dr. Chapman introducing the material they will study in the upcoming week.

6. You will close the session in prayer and send couples home to apply to their marriages what they are learning.

Each session is designed to last 60 to 90 minutes. You can customize the sessions to fit the amount of time your group has to meet. As a leader, you don't need to be an experienced marriage counselor or Bible scholar. You don't even need to have a perfect marriage. What *do* you need to lead this study?

**Personally:**
• A commitment to learn your spouse's love language and strengthen your own marriage.

- A passion for married couples to learn to love one another deeply and establish strong, healthy, lasting marriages.
- A belief in prayer and the power of God's Word to change lives.
- A desire for all persons to come to know God's love through Christ in a personal way.
- A commitment to complete each week's assignments before your small-group session. (You don't need to have all the answers, but you need to be familiar with the material.)

**For the Group:**

- A member book for each person (husbands and wives will need their own book)
- The Leader Kit with the DVDs and CD-ROM
- A small group of about six couples. This study is an excellent outreach tool that can improve marriages as well as bring people to a saving relationship with Jesus Christ. Encourage believers who plan to participate in the study to invite their non-churched friends to join you.
- A comfortable meeting place with access to a TV and DVD player. A home makes an ideal setting, especially if you intend to invite non-Christian couples to participate.
- Child care! This is essential! Perhaps your church has a child-care budget that you can use to pay child-care workers. You might ask each couple with children to pay a sum each session or pass around a basket each week and ask adults to donate to the child-care fund.

Remember, this leader guide is simply a guide and not a strict program to follow.

Enhance it and revise it with your own creativity to fit your group's needs and your leadership style. Always prepare spiritually for each session by committing your study to God in prayer.

## Session 1

BEFORE THE SESSION

1. Prepare a contact sheet for participants to write their names, addresses, phone numbers, and e-mail addresses. (You can use this information during the study to stay in touch with group members.) Place the contact sheet on a table near the entrance along with pens, markers, name tags, copies of the member book, and a basket for collecting money.
2. Print copies of "Love in Any Language" from the CD-ROM.
3. Print extra copies of the Session 1 Viewer Guide from the CD-ROM.
4. Prepare to show DVD Session 1: Learning to Speak Love.

DURING THE SESSION

1. As participants arrive, ask them to sign in, prepare name tags, and pick up copies of the member book. Invite them to leave payment for their books in the basket or offer to collect their money later.
2. Once participants sign in, hand each a copy of "Love in Any Language." Instruct them to write what language they think the words in that square represent.

3. Introduce yourself by sharing your name and wedding anniversary. Have your spouse share his or her name and how many years you have been married. Ask the other couples to introduce themselves in the same manner.

4. Ask group members to share their language guesses for the first square on "Love in Any Language." Identify the correct language.* Continue that process with all nine squares. Explain: *There are many ways to say "I love you," but we must say it in a language the other person can understand. In the upcoming weeks we will learn to say "I love you" in languages our spouses understand.*

5. Use the information on page 4 to introduce Dr. Gary Chapman. Read Dr. Chapman's warning for this study: "Understanding the five love languages and learning to speak the primary love language of your spouse may radically affect his or her behavior. People behave differently when their emotional love tanks are full."

6. Ask: *How many of you speak more than one language? Did you learn those languages as children or adults?* Say: *We absorb our native tongue with no effort, but as adults we have to* **choose** *to learn a new language and continuously practice speaking that language if we want to remain fluent. In the same way, adults who want to strengthen their marriages must* **choose** *to learn and continually practice speaking their spouse's love language.*

7. Explain that one way participants will demonstrate their commitment to learn their spouse's love language is by studying the member book. Invite members to flip through the member book as you explain the weekly format. Even though this book is not divided into individual days of study, encourage them to spread their study over the week rather than try to study everything in one sitting. Also encourage them to complete every activity to get the most out of their study. Some activities involve reading a Bible passage, most of which are printed in the margin. Participants will need to look up some passages in their Bibles. If there are unchurched adults in your small group, make sure everyone has a Bible and briefly explain how to find the passages. Assure participants that they will not be asked to share any personal evaluation activities. Remind them that everything discussed in your small group is confidential.

8. Explain that the video message will introduce the material they will be studying during the upcoming week. Have members turn to the viewer guide on page 7, or pass out copies of the viewer guide for Session 1 and invite them to take notes as they view the video. Play the Session 1 video (approx. 35 min).

9. Ask husbands and wives to pair up and share the most encouraging thing they heard on the video and what they most want to get out of this study. (Couple discussion suggestions can be printed off the CD-ROM.)

10. Share what you desire to see happen in this group and in their individual marriages as a result of this study. Assign the week 1 material

in the member book for the next group session.

11. Close in prayer, asking for God's blessings on each marriage represented as you learn to speak the five love languages.

\* Answers: 1. Yugoslavian; 2. German; 3. Swahili; 4. Burmese; 5. French; 6. Danish; 7. Lebanese; 8. Czech; 9. Spanish (from *www.800iloveyou.com/iloveyou.htm*).

## Session 2

### BEFORE THE SESSION

1. Provide name tags and markers.
2. Print copies of the Session 2 Viewer Guide from the CD-ROM.
3. Prepare to show DVD Session 2: Love Language One—Words of Affirmation.

### DURING THE SESSION

1. As participants arrive, ask them to wear name tags again this week.
2. Invite volunteers to share something funny that happened at their wedding. Ask: *After you were married, did you discover that marriage was different than what you anticipated? Explain.*
3. Use the following discussion starters:
   • What did Dr. Chapman say is a fundamental reason many couples find it nearly impossible to keep love alive in their marriages? What does he say is the key to a long-lasting, loving marriage? Are you beginning to agree with him?

   • Do you agree that *love* is the most important word in the English language? Explain. How does Ecclesiastes 4:9-12 express why all people have a deep desire to be intimate with others (p. 15)? What did God give us to meet that need for intimacy and love?

   • How did Dr. Chapman's illustration of the emotional love tank help you better understand your behavior and that of others? Do you think it will cost you more to fill your car's gas tank or your spouse's love tank? Explain. Will it be worth it? How?

   • What do you think, or know, is your primary love language? What most helped you make that discovery the questions in this week's study or the profile?

   • What if your spouse's love language doesn't come naturally to you (p. 14)? How is true love a completely unselfish emotion and action?

4. Ask husbands and wives to pair up. Instruct them to share their responses to the love tank activity on page 10. Encourage them to compare but not despair if one or both love tanks are running on empty. God can use this study to fill their love tanks and turn their marriages around. Next, ask couples to share, one at a time, what they believe to be their primary love language and then what they believe to be their spouse's primary love language (couple discussion suggestions also on CD-ROM).

5. Call couples back to the large group and have

members turn to the viewer guide on page 23, or pass out copies of the video viewer guide for Session 2. Play the Session 2 video (approx. 15 min).

6. Encourage couples to make a deliberate choice to fill their spouse's love tank this week. Remind them of the "Tank Check" game Dr. Chapman spoke of in his message this week. Challenge them to play the game throughout the study. Encourage participants to interact with the material in the member book for the next group session.

7. Close in prayer, thanking God for the gift of His love and asking for His power to learn to speak one another's love language.

## Session 3

### BEFORE THE SESSION

1. Print copies of the Session 3 Viewer Guide from the CD-ROM.
2. Prepare to show DVD Session 3: Love Language Two—Quality Time.

### DURING THE SESSION

1. Ask: *How did you behave or think differently this week because of your awareness of love tanks and love languages?*
2. Ask: *What do you think is the most powerful muscle in the human body? Why? How can such a small portion of our bodies have such a large impact on our marriages?*
3. Use the following discussion starters:

- Use the first activity on page 24 to compare the positive and negative effects of words.
- Give examples of verbal compliments we can use to build up our mates. How can we avoid insincere flattery in our attempts to learn the dialect of verbal compliments? How can we respond positively to our spouses' attempts to give us verbal compliments?
- According to Scripture, what can be accomplished in our mates if we speak love to them through encouraging words (p. 26)? What's the difference between encouraging words and verbal pressure (aka: nagging)? What is required in order to give our spouses encouraging words? Give examples of encouraging words we can offer our mates.
- What's the relationship between kind words and patience (p. 28)? What besides actual words is involved in speaking kindness? Read Proverbs 15:1. Give examples of statements that can be either gentle or harsh based on the tone of voice. (For example: "Glad to see you took out the trash." "Are you picking up Susie today?")
- If we are going to commit to speak kind words to our spouses, what must we do with the pains and failures of the past? To what extent are we to forgive our spouses according to Ephesians 4:32 and Colossians 3:12-13 (p. 28-29)? What does that mean?
- Why is humility essential for a loving marriage? Give examples of humble words.
- Did you start a notebook of affirming

words? What are some of your favorites?

- Have you ever been the recipient of indirect words of affirmation? How did that make you feel? Do you prefer to receive direct words of affirmation from your spouse or to overhear your spouse brag on you to another person?

4. Encourage husbands and wives to pair up and speak words of affirmation directly to one another by looking into their spouse's eyes and speaking the words they wrote in the apple on page 31. Then ask them to share the positive traits they wrote in the margin on page 30. Finally, ask them to discuss what other encouraging words they would like to hear (see the activity at the top of p. 31; couple discussion suggestions also on CD-ROM).

5. Affirm participants for their willingness to apply what they are learning to strengthen their marriages. Have members turn to the viewer guide on page 35, or pass out copies of the video viewer guide for Session 3. Play the Session 3 video (approx. 19 min).

6. Encourage couples to continue speaking Words of Affirmation in the next week even as they study Quality Time. Explain that they will have an opportunity next session to share the differences they have observed in their marriages after speaking affirming words to their spouses. Assign the week 3 material in the member book for the next group session.

7. Close in prayer, asking God to help each of you use His gift of words to build up one another and your marriages.

# Session 4

## BEFORE THE SESSION

1. Prepare a display of valuable items including a clock, money (and/or credit cards), jewelry, electronic items.

2. Print copies of the Session 4 Viewer Guide from the CD-ROM.

3. Prepare the DVD to show Session 4: Love Language Three—Receiving Gifts.

## DURING THE SESSION

1. Invite volunteers to share differences they observed in themselves and their marriages when they chose to daily speak Words of Affirmation to their spouses.

2. Draw attention to your display of valuable items. Ask group members which of the items represent commodities that are valuable to them. Ask: *Would you choose to have more time or money? Why? Why is giving quality time a powerful way to speak love to your spouse?*

3. Use the following discussion starters:

- What does it mean to give someone quality time? What percentage of the day would you estimate most husbands and wives give each other undivided attention? What do you think would happen in marriages if spouses upped that time by just 10 percent?

- Do you think it is childish to need someone's undivided attention or is it a legitimate adult need? Explain.

- Give examples of a normal conversation that

takes place in your house on a daily basis. What is quality conversation? How comfortable are you with quality conversation? What should we do if sympathetic dialogue makes us uncomfortable but Quality Time is our spouses' primary love language?

• Read Proverbs 20:5 (p. 37-38). How can we be men or women of understanding who draw out the depths in our mates' hearts?

• What two actions are involved in quality conversation? Read 2 Corinthians 6:11-13. What is your spouse requesting when he or she asks you to share your thoughts and feelings (p. 39)? If your love language dialect is quality conversation and your spouse's is not, identify good and bad times to ask your spouse to share his or her deepest self with you.

• From last weeks video, are you a Dead Sea or Babbling Brook? Do you need to listen more or talk more?

4. Ask couples to pair up and share the five things they would like to do together (p. 40). Give them time to compile the list of six activities they will do together in the coming months. Ask them to make a full list even if they are uncertain of dates or available funds. They can go back and revise the list later (couple discussion suggestions also on CD-ROM).

5. After giving couples time to discuss their lists, call them back to the large group. Have members turn to the viewer guide on page 45, or pass out copies of the video viewer guide for Session 4. Play the Session 4 video (approx. 18 min).

6. Affirm participants for the quality time they are giving to their personal study and to your small-group time. Assign the week 4 material in the member book for the next group session.

7. Read Psalm 31:15a and pray, thanking God for the gift of time and asking Him to help couples use their time wisely to speak love to one another.

## Session 5

BEFORE THE SESSION

1. Obtain a small gift for each participant such as a candy bar or a goodie bag of fun treats.

2. Print copies of the Session 5 Viewer Guide from the CD-ROM.

3. Prepare to show DVD Session 5: Love Language Four—Acts of Service.

DURING THE SESSION

1. Ask volunteers to share how they spent quality time with their spouses the past week. Invite those who participated in the optional activity at the end of Week 3 (p. 41) to briefly describe how they presented the romantic invitation to their spouse and what response they received. (Nothing too personal, please!)

2. Distribute the gifts to each participant. Ask them to share how they feel about receiving a gift, even a small one, and why. Explain: *Everyone likes to receive gifts, but for those whose primary love language is Receiving*

*Gifts, the best part of the gift is not the item itself but the feeling of love the gift expresses. Why do gifts convey love so powerfully?*

3. Use the following discussion starters:

   • Do you agree or disagree that love is always accompanied by giving? Why? Read John 3:16. Identify the Gift, Giver, and reason for the gift.

   • When it comes to giving, is it really only the thought that counts? Explain.

   • Share ideas for inexpensive or free gifts that convey the message, "I love you." According to 2 Corinthians 8:12, what is the key to expressing love through gift giving (p. 47)?

   • Read Proverbs 11:24-25. Describe a time when giving or receiving refreshed you. How have you observed your spouse being refreshed by giving or receiving gifts?

   • What might you need to change if you are going to effectively speak love through gifts? How difficult would that be for you? How can savers who seek to be financially responsible for their families still be givers?

   • What if/then statements did you pull out of Luke 6:38 (p. 50)? How have you personally observed the truth of that verse?

   • How is the gift of presence different from the love language Quality Time, or is it the same? How can we know if our spouse wants our presence or wants to be left alone?

4. Ask couples to pair up and share with one another how they completed the statements requesting their desire for their spouse's presence (p. 50). Then direct them to ask: *Is the amount of gifts I give you too little, too much, or just right? How can I more clearly speak love to you through giving?* (couple discussion suggestions also on CD-ROM).

5. Invite participants back to the large group. Have members turn to the viewer guide on page 55, or pass out copies of the video viewer guide for Session 5. Play the Session 5 video (approx. 12 min).

6. Assign the week 5 material in the member book for the next group session.

7. Read 2 Corinthians 8:7. Pray, thanking God for demonstrating His love through the gift of His Son and asking for His help to excel in the love language of receiving gifts.

## Session 6

### BEFORE THE SESSION

1. On one wall in the meeting space display a small placard reading, "Torture." On another wall display a placard reading, "Love."

2. Be aware that Session 7 is the last video session. Plan to discuss with your small-group if they would like to go ahead and meet for one final time to discuss the material in Week 7 of the member book or wrap up the study after Session 7. If you choose to meet one final time, you might plan a potluck meal or dessert at that meeting. (It is probably not the best idea to meet at a restaurant since you need privacy and few distractions for the discussion.)

3. Print copies of the Session 6 Viewer Guide

from the CD-ROM.

4. Prepare to show DVD Session 6: Love Language Five—Physical Touch.

DURING THE SESSION

1. Invite volunteers to share how they expressed love to their spouse through a creatively inexpensive gift this past week.

2. Explain that you are going to make a series of statements such as, "To me, washing dishes is …" They are to stand next to the placard (either "Torture" or "Love") that best finishes each statement for them. They can stand in the middle of the room if their response to that act of service depends on the circumstances. Read a series of statements involving common chores such as: "To me, taking the car to the shop is … Vacuuming is … Bathing the baby is … Cooking a meal is …"

3. After a few minutes of this game (make it fun!) ask group members what they can discern about one another based on the side of the room they most often went to. Ask: *Why is Acts of Service, especially if it's not your love language, such a powerful communicator of love in marriage?*

4. Use the following discussion starters:
   • If you found yourself in the middle of the room during the prior activity, what were the circumstances that determined whether or not your service was torture or a sign of love? What is the key to making Acts of Service a way to speak love rather than a dreaded chore?
   • What did you learn about service from Jesus' example (p. 56-57)? Did it surprise you that the purpose of One so great was to serve others? What does that teach us about how to truly be great in this world and specifically in our homes?
   • Read the quote in the margin on page 57. What do you think that means? How do we lose our focus in marriage and start demanding instead of making requests? How can we regain our focus so we can serve one another in love?
   • Read Colossians 3:23-24. Whether or not Acts of Service is your primary love language, how can living this passage improve your service toward your spouse (p. 58)?
   • How can viewing your most dreaded chore as a sign of love and an investment in your marriage change your whole attitude toward service?

5. Ask couples to pair up and compare their lists of what they can do for one another that would demonstrate their love (p. 57). Encourage them to honestly discuss whether those are reasonable requests and to keep working this week until they have lists agreeable to both of them (couple discussion suggestions also on CD-ROM).

6. Have members turn to the viewer guide on page 63, or pass out copies of the video viewer guide for Session 6. Play the Session 6 video (approx. 18 min).

7. Urge couples to lovingly perform an act of service for their spouse each day this week. Assign the week 6 material in the member book for the next group session.

8. Close in prayer, asking God to help couples serve one another in love.

## Session 7

### BEFORE THE SESSION

1. If you are going to have a final small-group meeting after Session 7, be prepared to finalize those plans this week. If this will be your last small-group meeting, try to plan something special for the couples.

2. Print copies of the Session 7 Viewer Guide from the CD-ROM.

3. Prepare to show DVD Session 7: Growing in Love.

### DURING THE SESSION

1. Invite participants to share how their spouse performed an act of service for them this past week and how that service made them feel loved.

2. Ask why physical touch is such a powerful communicator of love. Discuss the mysteries of emotion as related to physical touch. For example, at times our emotional tanks crave an embrace when we hurt; but at other times we don't want to be touched at all. Moods, attitudes, and perceptions all affect whether we desire to be touched, held, or have sex on

a given occasion.

3. Use the following discussion starters:
   - Read Mark 10:13-16. Do you agree or disagree that children are in greater need of loving physical touch than adults? Why?
   - When are physical touches not loving? How can we discern what is loving and what is bothersome to our mates?
   - How did 1 Corinthians 7:3-5 challenge you to treat your spouse's body (p. 66)? How does this verse relate to even the comments you make about your spouse's body?
   - Were you surprised to find verses about intimate touch in the Bible? What does God desire for your marriage in terms of loving physical touch (pp. 66-67)? (Example: God wants you to enjoy loving intimate physical touch with your spouse and *only* with your spouse.)

4. As you move into the couple discussion time, ask couples to spread out more than usual so they can have more privacy. First, ask them to compare their responses to the activities of the week on page 64 to discover how important physical touch is to each of them. Then ask them to discuss the final activity of the week and follow the instructions to pray together (p. 69; couple discussion suggestions also on CD-ROM).

5. Give couples time to discuss and then ask everyone to come back to the large group. Have members turn to the viewer guide on page 73, or pass out copies of the video viewer guide for Session 7. Play the

Session 7 video (approx. 36 min).

6. Assign the week 7 material in the member book for the next group session. If you have chosen not to meet to discuss Week 7, encourage group members to complete their study in the member book and to continue applying what they have learned from *The Five Love Languages* to their marriages. Thank them for their participation and faithfulness to this study.

7. Close in prayer, thanking God for touching you with His love and asking Him to help you bring His healing touch to your marriages.

## Session 8 [OPTIONAL; NO VIDEO SEGMENT]

### BEFORE THE SESSION

1. Make any necessary arrangements if you are having a fellowship during this session.

2. Print out copies of "My Commitment to You" from the CD-ROM (on parchment paper if possible).

### DURING THE SESSION

1. Discuss: *In Week 6 we were challenged to identify how we could provide loving touches to those who need them. How did you find ways to express love to others through touch and what responses did you receive?*

2. Ask: *What is meant by "Love is blind"? When do a man and woman who are in love begin to see one another in a more realistic light?*

3. Use the following discussion starters:

- How did you first think, feel, and act when you began to fall in love with your spouse? If you don't have that giddy "in-love" feeling anymore, does that mean you no longer love one another? Explain.

- What did Dr. Chapman say is the faulty information that trips up married couples? Why is it a good thing we don't remain obsessed with our loved one?

- Read the idealistic version of love in the "paraphrase" of 1 Corinthians 13 on page 77. Replace it with the description of real love. Which type of love is based on how you feel? On what is true love based?

- According to the psychologists cited, how is the "in-love" experience different from real love? According to 1 John 3:16,18, how is the "in-love" experience different from real love (p. 78)? Give practical examples of how we can daily lay down our lives for our spouses.

- Is real love an emotion, choice, action, attitude, or all of the above? Explain. Why is love that grows out of reason and choice, rather than instinct and chemistry, a more satisfying and fulfilling love?

- Is it disappointing or encouraging to discover it is OK to not have those giddy, obsessive, "in-love" emotions now that you're married? Why? Does that mean real, enduring love can't be exciting? Explain.

- At the beginning of our study, Dr. Chapman warned us that understanding the five love languages and learning to speak the primary love language of our spouses may radically affect their behavior. How have you personally experienced that truth during the past few weeks?

- What is the most valuable lesson you have gained from this study?

4. Instruct husbands and wives to pair up and share differences they have observed in each other and in their marriage because of their study of *The Five Love Languages*. Ask them to thank their spouses for the ways they have spoken their love language and discuss ways they can better speak each other's love language in the years to come (couple discussion suggestions also on CD-ROM).

5. Distribute the "My Commitment to You" handouts. Encourage participants to either sign that commitment and present it to their spouse at this time, to reaffirm their commitment if they have already completed the activity on page 80, or to make firm plans to present that commitment this week. Suggest they revisit this commitment every two months to make sure they are staying on track with speaking one another's love language.

6. Read 1 John 4:9-10. Explain that the only way anyone can truly experience and express love is by having an intimate love relationship with Jesus Christ. If you have non-churched couples in your group, share how to have a personal relationship with Christ. (Use the special video message from Dr. Chapman called "The Ultimate Expression of Love" [approx. 4 min.] to help you with this.) Invite participants to share if they have received Christ as a result of this study and rejoice with them. Encourage adults who would like to know more about accepting Christ to speak with you after the session.

7. Close in prayer, thanking God for the gift of love. Ask Him to help each couple be an example of true, abiding love to one another and to the world.

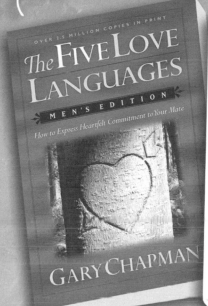
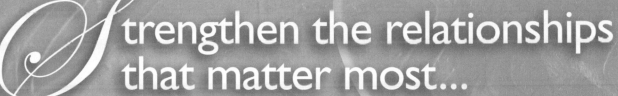
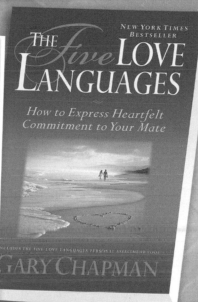

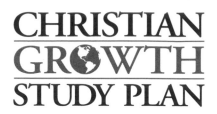

# CHRISTIAN GROWTH STUDY PLAN

In the **Christian Growth Study Plan**, *The Five Love Languages* is a resource for course credit in the subject area Home and Family of the Christian Growth category of plans. To receive credit, read the book, complete the learning activities, show your work to your pastor, a staff member or church leader, then complete the following information. This page may be duplicated. Send the completed page to:

**Christian Growth Study Plan**
**One LifeWay Plaza; Nashville, TN 37234-0117**
**FAX: (615)251-5067; E-mail:** *cgspnet@lifeway.com*
For information about the Christian Growth Study Plan, refer to the Christian Growth Study Plan Catalog online at *www.lifeway.com/cgsp*. If you do not have access to the Internet, contact the Christian Growth Study Plan office (1.800.968.5519) for the specific plan you need for your ministry.

## The Five Love Languages
### CG-0196

### PARTICIPANT INFORMATION

Social Security Number (USA ONLY-optional)  |  Personal CGSP Number*  |  Date of Birth (MONTH, DAY, YEAR)

Name (First, Middle, Last)  |  Home Phone

Address (Street, Route, or P.O. Box)  |  City, State, or Province  |  Zip/Postal Code

Email Address for CGSP use

Please check appropriate box:  ❏ Resource purchased by church  ❏ Resource purchased by self  ❏ Other

### CHURCH INFORMATION

Church Name

Address (Street, Route, or P.O. Box)  |  City, State, or Province  |  Zip/Postal Code

### CHANGE REQUEST ONLY

☐ Former Name

☐ Former Address  |  City, State, or Province  |  Zip/Postal Code

☐ Former Church  |  City, State, or Province  |  Zip/Postal Code

Signature of Pastor, Conference Leader, or Other Church Leader  |  Date

*New participants are requested but not required to give SS# and date of birth.  Existing participants, please give CGSP# when using SS# for the first time.  Thereafter, only one ID# is required.  **Mail to:** Christian Growth Study Plan, One LifeWay Plaza, Nashville, TN 37234-0117. Fax: (615)251-5067.

Revised 4-05